The Matrix of Four

The Philosophy of The Duality of Polarity

By Ethan Indigo Smith

~Dedicated to the fourth wise monkey, the righteous rebels.

"First they laugh at you, then they ignore you, then they fight you, then you win."

~Attributed to Mahatmas Gandhi

Contents

Introduction to Absolutes

Quotes of Contrast

Introduction to Absolutes

The Matrix of Four, The Philosophy of the Duality of Polarity is a philosophy applicable to numerous and diverse subjects. The Matrix of Four is metaphysics and philosophy, it is metaphilosophy combining thinking models into a thinking model. It is metaphilosophy providing and linking diversity into mutuality. When I first began writing it I originally thought I invented the concept, but soon realized my expression of it was just a small part of a much bigger and ancient idea.

The Matrix of Four, The Philosophy of The Duality of Polarity inevitably develops individual awareness and consciousness. It can also instigate and enhance one's intuition and understanding thereof. The formula is applicable to, and assists understanding of politics, science, theology, mathematics, reason, debate, meditation and innumerable structures and systems. The idea has also proven to be, perhaps most importantly, highly inspirational.

I utilized the metaphilosophy for years, as you no doubt have too. I referenced it repeatedly, I presented nuanced thoughts composed by way of it, but I was, for all extents and purposes, unaware of its specifics until I began to write and research another idea. The Matrix of Four is a philosopher's tool used constantly in rhetoric and logic, yet it most often goes unmentioned and unseen. Metaphilosophy is like that, present yet silent, permeating so many subjects and objects as to be practically unnoticed. The Matrix of Four is ever present and yet elusive, and in some circles aspects of it have even been variously hidden and suppressed.

I initially conceptualized a set of four concerning our thinking and being in the political spectrum. In The Complete Patriot's Guide to Oligarchical Collectivism I posit there are four political archetypes; Idiots, Zealots, Elitists and Patriots. I proposed this set in order to understand individuals and bypass traditional prejudiced labels. The deciding factor in this matrix is individual reaction to information. Idiots don't question relevance, finding comfort in their ignorance. Zealots question limitedly, in accordance to their preconceptions. Elitists question in order to advance their power and do not share information. Patriots question and share information openly.

These four base political archetypes correlate with Gandhi's quote used as the epigraph for this book, and much more. Idiots laugh, Zealots ignore, Elitists war, and Patriots win peace, through peace. The epigraph suggests there are four stages of reaction, and also four types of reactionaries. Gandhi had new ideas which were difficult for people to accept in a feudal world, and I suspect he knew all about how individuals react to new ideas and new information.

Gandhi was a Patriot among Idiots, Zealots and Elitists. My definition of a Patriot is more comparable to a peaceful activist or inactivist, like Gandhi, not a nationalist, or jingoist, or uniformed institutional representative as is often the cliché. Perhaps my definition of patriotism would be best expressed as matriotism, of open maternal love for locals, land and liberty, as opposed to the blind loyalty to patriarchal, martial institutions that patriotism is mostly associated with.

The matrix of political thinking and being mirrored many other ideas, Gandhi's point for instance and also subtle layers in George Orwell's *1984*, the inspiration for my first book The Complete Patriot's Guide to Oligarchical Collectivism. There are clearly, though subtly, four classes of people described in this epic and influential political fiction; the Inner Party, the Outer Party, the Proles and the Brotherhood. George also implies there is a tendency to portray three rather than four, through the suggested elimination of the Brotherhood from the story.

The first sentence from what is known as the book within the book in *1984*, titled The Theory and Practice of Oligarchical Collectivism, curiously states there are three types of people in the world, "Throughout recorded time, and probably since the end of the Neolithic Age there have been three kinds of people in the world, the High, the Middle and the Low."

One layer of *1984* concerns the elimination of language and words, while another reveals there are four parts and that there is an inclination to eliminate the distinct fourth part. In reality, for many different reasons, aspects of the truth are removed akin to the outright elimination of language. And in reality, the fourth part of many sets is often eliminated or unsaid as well as being the distinct part of the set.

Judging people as high, middle and low is unfair and ridiculous. George was well aware of this. However understanding people according to how they react to information is possibly the most accurate and fair way to understand people. The specifics of thinking and being are difficult to view and quantify, but how people react to specific information is one clear window. We either ignore relevant information, we choose what we want to ignore to maintain view, we use information for our own gains, or we openly accept and share information for all to prosper, no matter.

The Idiots, Zealots, Elitists and Patriots set is a fair way to understand political thinking and being based on our reaction to information, and via the matrix of four, it's complete. I limitedly applied the metaphilosophy, as many have before me, to politics. I was basically unknowingly influenced by it and conjured my own set of four utilizing it, and yet still didn't recognize even the entire silhouette of the idea. I felt there was more to four, I just had no idea how much more there was. I had been struck by The Matrix of Four, The Philosophy of The Duality of Polarity, but had yet to even come up with the term to describe it. Sometimes philosophy and invention is like that, an intuitive course before becoming a recognized route.

Over time I realized there were so many examples of the formula, that it was a matrix applicable to everything from political observation to personal meditation, that it was a true metaphilosophy, not limited to just political science. Politics finds its way into everything, even philosophy, even supposed science, so as to influence political thinking using what is politically steering. My observations of politics, specifically the thinking and being of individuals and institutions, led me to the metaphilosophy that is partly political, being metaphilosophy, but is based on scientific absolutes, and not politics at all.

As the metaphilosophy coalesced into focus I found the words to express the concept, the title to the book. There wasn't one moment where I had an epiphany of sorts, but rather several when mathematical and spiritual concepts left me stunned. I still occasionally encounter new powerful ideas reflective of the Matrix of Four and I constantly utilize it to form accurate observations. The metaphilosophy is mathematical and numerological, but goes beyond the numerical comparative too.

Every time I learn a new way to utilize the matrix or another way it has been utilized before, I experience what I have come to call shivers of signification. Usually these arrive from ancient ideas that almost become a matrix onto themselves, aspects of an idea that all point to an idea I simply recognized and clarified.

The Matrix of Four, The Philosophy of The Duality of Polarity is metaphilosophy based on absolutes, and yet as metaphilosophy, it is not an absolute in itself. It cannot be. Ultimately this is not a flaw, for the philosophies and doctrines presented as absolute infallible models have consistently been the most flawed and most dangerous ideas to be put forth.

Metaphilosophy has to be applicable to everything from meditation, or individual consciousness, to consideration of politics, or mass consciousness, a mirror reflecting the inner and outer world, joining object and subject. It should be based on absolutes, and yet in order to remain unflawed, metaphilosophy must have what some might consider one flaw, that it not be a rigid absolute itself. Valid metaphilosophy is like Native American Indian rug, bowl and basket weaving patterns. Each design is perfect, except for one purposefully included skip in the pattern, so as to give the design freedom.

With each shiver of signification the metaphilosophy became clearer and expanded. So many absolutes were composed of it and so much theosophy celebrated it, that I realized the idea could not be my own. I noticed it, I elaborated and focused on different aspects of it, but the idea is ancient and is not simply my own. It is a vibration. I am just a transmitter of the idea, of a mandala or the mandala, a topic at times resembling an elusive and rumored golden correlative, or philosophy of everything. The concept is so widely shared I quickly found validation of the Idiots, Zealots, Elitists and Patriots set, and eventually, more importantly, found the metaphilosophy, the omnipresence of which ultimately illustrates the brotherhood of man, and the righteous rebel, and the concept of nullisis, and inspiration for enhanced awareness.

The presence of the metaphilosophy is so overwhelming that it is impossible to deny its existence and its influence. The Matrix of Four is bigger than a mere conjured idea, or numerological abstract celebrated among diverse cultures. It may be beyond a human idea, rather something we noticed, being at the basis of so many objects and subjects, including so many absolutes. Some of those who pondered it before, like Gandhi, Orwell, Herman Hesse, Carl Jung, Socrates and countless others were probably acutely aware of it, others might have been simply under its influence, while many might have actively tried to keep it hidden for one reason or another. The metaphilosophy is rooted in science, mathematics, philosophy, theology and is not a numerical conjuration, but a metaphysical and metaphilosophical recognition.

This metaphilosophy elevates individual and collective consciousness. Consciousness is simply the awareness of awareness. And though for most analytical purposes it is intangible, consciousness has been proven to have real effects on the outcome of scientific experiments. It is commonly understood that our consciousness can instigate healing inside of us. The notion of the Placebo Effect acknowledges the power of consciousness to gain relief and spur healing through meditative imagination. It's spiritually accepted and scientifically validated that we can change ourselves as well as circumstances outside of ourselves through the power of our consciousness. Consciousness is everywhere, comparable to gravity in its reach, intangibility and unwavering power.

The Matrix of Four, The Philosophy of The Duality of Polarity began for me with the idea of Idiots, Zealots, Elitists and Patriots. This set of four towards understanding how we react to new information can enhance the awareness of our consciousness. As a metaphilosophy however the basis of The Matrix of Four begins with and is based on some of the most poignant and inarguable absolutes in the universe. It is based on four all-encompassing absolutes, a primal set of four, each reflective of or made up of a matrix of four on its own, each birthing and birthed from the same vibration matrix. The four primal absolutes are used as the basis for the Matrix of Four, but in fact numerous related absolutes are intertwined with each absolute forming the basis for the metaphilosophy.

The primal set of four makes up the basic aspects of reality, each composed of an absolute in the form of, or forming, a matrix of four. The idea of mind/body/spirit reflects a trinity lacking the fourth part, the universe, or nature. The universal is the missing fourth aspect in mind, body spirit idea. This fourfold aspect of reality in this respect is the mental, the physical, the spiritual and universal surroundings. The Matrix of Four, The Philosophy of The Duality of Polarity is based on mental, physical, spiritual and universal/natural absolutes comparable to the trinity of mind, body, spirit, only with the lacking fourth part included. The spiritual absolute of The Matrix of Four, related to consciousness, is the distinct one of the set in that it has not been scientifically validated as absolute being spiritual, but is based on ideas so ancient that it's comparably inarguable as much as many scientific observations.

The Matrix of Four, The Philosophy of the Duality of Polarity is based on inarguable absolutes, like two plus two equals four. It is applicable to and helpful with diverse matters, but it is not an absolute in and of itself. Philosophy of merit should have absolutes or ideas approaching such at the basis, and yet no philosophy is absolute, no matter if otherwise presented.

There are very few absolutes in the universe and the Matrix of Four is based on four of the most primal absolutes of the highest order reflective of mind, body, spirit and nature. The Matrix of Four is based on absolutes, but this is no absolutist manifesto, and one should never trust a philosophy presenting itself as an absolute for even the following metaphilosophy based on four of the most primal absolutes of all existence is not an absolute.

The Matrix of Four, The Philosophy of The Duality of Polarity is useful in understanding meditation and political situations, individual and collective consciousness. It enables understanding of the connection between the macrocosm and the microcosm, the inner and outer worlds. It links science with spirituality, mathematics with the symbolic, and it transforms diversity into commonality. It is useful in honing one's communication skills, one's intuitive capability, observation skills and in expanding one's perspective on everything from quiet breathing to the ruckus of politics.

The Matrix of Four, The Philosophy of The Duality of Polarity is a highly elusive and yet totally ubiquitous, frequently suggested, now clarified metaphilosophy that proves the brotherhood of man and at the same time presents a way of thinking to uplift the brotherhood of man. The formula can be used for social and political problem solving, like arithmetic is used for mathematical problem solving. In fact, The Matrix of Four is born from the same womb as the absolute of arithmetic at the basis of all mathematics.

The first absolute is a result of perhaps the most constant absolute across the entire universe. All absolutes are arguable spare an elect few. And the Matrix of Four, The Philosophy of The Duality of Polarity begins in the most primal and inarguable of absolutes. All things are in flux and even the stars are finite making absolutes rare. And yet some things are the same here as they are everywhere else in the dynamic and dramatic universe, now and X billion years ago.

All of mathematics, in its infinite complexity, is based on the four operations of arithmetic. This set of four, of two contrasting pairs of opposing operations is exactly depictive of the duality of polarity. Arithmetic exists completely in the mind, a mental intangible, yet it is still represents invaluable absolutes. All of mathematics is based on addition, subtraction, multiplication and division in duality of polarity. All further mathematical formulas are simply different combinations and variations of the four operations of arithmetic. Mathematics is the most reliable and valuable subject in the universe and is based on two pairs of contrasting operations in duality of polarity.

The second absolute at the basis of The Matrix of Four is born of the natural absolute of gravity and the resulting coming and going of celestial objects in orbit. Gravity is one of the four known forces of the universe among a theorized five forces. Electromagnetism is another one of the four forces. Electromagnetic force depicts the Matrix of Four and The Philosophy of The Duality of Polarity exactly in the positive and negative flows of electric magnetic current.

All objects in orbit of other celestial bodies experience four phases in their spherical revolutions. The elliptical rotation of orbiting spheres crossing space results in winter and summer solstices and vernal and autumnal equinoxes all across creation. This primary set of four, of two contrasting pairs in the form of the duality of polarity, is an undeniable absolute of unfathomable proportions. The greatest celestial bodies, the most tangible objects in the universe all experience two equinoxes and two solstices, exactly depictive of the duality of polarity. Gravity results in the related four seasons here on Earth and everywhere. The four seasons of spheres in motion is the greatest absolute across the universe and results in the constant physical expression of the duality of polarity.

The Matrix of Four, The Philosophy of The Duality of Polarity is birthed from, based on and reflects the universal absolutes of orbit and arithmetic. These absolutes are the basis for more knowledge and discovery than perhaps any other absolutes or knowledge whatsoever. Through understanding the four seasons and four operations of arithmetic people have traversed the globe and invented different ways of doing so. The Matrix of Four, The Philosophy of The Duality of Polarity is derived from these primal absolutes and can similarly assist understanding a wide array of objects and subjects, the same way as knowledge of seasons and arithmetic leads to other understandings.

The metaphilosophy begins in macrocosmic absolutes. Throughout the book independent philosophies containing elements of the matrix are explored to illustrate various ways it can be utilized in life, in thinking and being, as arithmetic is used in mathematics. The philosophy and theology discussed are all debatable, and being that it is a way of thinking The Duality of Polarity itself is arguable, but the Duality of Polarity is based on inarguable and primal absolutes. It is extrapolated and depicted in the philosophy and theology of diverse peoples so extensively as to point to commonality in our thinking, the brotherhood of man.

The theology discussed is not reasoning for one to yield to a religious institution or belief system of any sort. In fact the theology is meant to build individuation and expand consciousness, not inspire institutional enrollment. The theology represents the extensive reach of the Matrix of Four, The Philosophy of The Duality of Polarity and I mean only respectful admiration to all theological ideas, however the following does not endorse or pay homage to any institution, including religious ones.

The metaphilosophy is one way of understanding objects and subjects and of linking the microcosmic with the macrocosmic. It is not the only, nor is it the best philosophical model for every situation, but it is a mathematically sound, physically proven, scientifically and logically sound way to reach clear understanding in most any situation. And sometimes it is among the few modes that remain sensible at all.

The Matrix of Four, The Philosophy of the Duality of Polarity might be recognizable to you, and it may have been hinted at before and explicitly unsaid until now. It is based on the greatest absolute among objects in the universe and the surest absolute of subjects; orbit and arithmetic. And yet it is metaphilosophy, a thinking model, not an absolute solution pertaining to every single dilemma. There are many ways to contemplate objects and subjects.

Many systems are undeniably related to The Matrix of Four, The Philosophy of The Duality of Polarity, whether initially noticed or not, however some are not at all. In numerology four is symbolic for completion and a balanced basis, but the first lesson of the metaphilosophy of the duality of polarity is deduction of its applicability.

The physical and tangible universe is in a constantly polarized state. Polarity is obvious and endless; there is activity and stillness, inside and outside, male and female, inhalation and exhalation, positive and negative, light and dark, expansion and contraction, passion and compassion, order and chaos, creation and destruction, birth and death, spirit and matter. Polarity is part of the natural order of the universe as we know it, and it is part of our social order as well; there's rich and poor, peace and war, rural and urban, formal and informal, serenity and calamity, acceptable and unacceptable, individuals and institutions, just and unjust, true and false. We polarize objects and subjects and yet many systems perceived as polarized are actually systems of degrees. Polarity occurs so frequently we often place it inaccurately, as well as often missing the obscured duality of polarity.

Some presentations of polarization are totally inaccurate. Perhaps the greatest social polarity, ever constant, ever conjured and nearly always incorrect is the idea of us and them. Social polarizations often result from the influences of naturally occurring polarity in combination with active manmade suggestions that such concepts have legitimate basis. Sometimes polarization is promoted and used to instigate the idea of us and them so as to divide and conquer. Sometimes people instigate false notions of us and them using doublespeak to make gains from such separation. Polarity is everywhere naturally, conceptually and sometimes unknowingly utilized unreasonably to separate and limit us. The Matrix of Four, The Philosophy of The Duality of Polarity is not doublespeak, it is not a suggestion of us and them, and it is not for separation, but for unification.

People polarize frequently and inaccurately to the point they contradict themselves and separate ideas, and even other people without noticing it. The Duality of Polarity is for contrast and inclusion. Polarity is ubiquitous, but this does not mean the social polarity of us and them, or any divisional concepts remotely resemble reasonable. Thinking in polarized terms is a vice when done to separate, and a virtue when utilized to unite. The polarization of us and them is an unreasonable polarization and often implemented from fear. The Matrix of Four is based on mutual conceptuality. The metaphilosophy unites through contrasts, and ultimately instigates understanding of the brotherhood of humanity.

The sheer frequency of polarity is influential enough to steer polarized thought without realization of it. When polarization is unknowingly engaged one separates the whole, undermining and limiting understanding. When polarization is noticed and understood as contrasting parts, enhanced understanding of the whole is initiated. The frequency of naturally occurring polarity is influential, but the significance of the objects and subjects in polarity is perhaps a more powerful reason for polarized thinking to be so commonplace it goes unnoticed. Societal polarization has little to do with the Duality of Polarity and might be instigated at the slightest suggestion when unaware.

The most influential orbs in the solar system from our earthly perspective, The Sun and Moon, are polarized. This polarity is just one of many primordial, influential and natural polarities. The Earth exists in a constantly polarized state of day and night. And yet this universal polarity exists completely in duality of polarity. There is the polarity of night and day and the duality of polarity with dawn and dusk, throughout the universe.

If one were to spend a year at The North Pole one year would be like one coming and going of the sun, one day. The vernal equinox would be like dawn. Night, day, dawn and dusk, are the four parts of one day in the formation of the duality of polarity and reflective of the four seasons of a year.

The Matrix of Four, The Philosophy of the Duality of Polarity is useful in understanding the basis of totality and instigating awareness of potentials. Polarity is so universally ubiquitous in reality as well as relativity, the whole idea is so invasive, especially when unconsidered, that people often conceptualize polarity where it does not exist, as a way to understand without realization they are doing so in a limiting manner. The metaphilosophy heightens awareness so one isn't steered to unnecessarily separate, or miss the potential subtle duality of polarity.

There is no physically distinct polarity in temperature, only in our perception of it. Temperature is measured by degrees. There is only a perceived and relative polarity of hot and cold. This is indicative of the tendency to polarize even in a displaced fashion, even if to accurately communicate relativity among a set of degrees. Nowhere in the universe is there a source of cold. Stars and planets provide and exchange heat, but there is no source of cold. There is only heat and its lacking by degrees. In such systems of degrees polarity is based on perspective and extremes. It's theorized the universe can all only be so cold; absolute zero being about -460 degrees Fahrenheit, and that there might be no limit to heat.

The idea of density is similarly inaccurately polarized according to our perception of soft and hard. Softness and hardness are used to communicate relativity and yet density is measured in degrees and not polarity. Singular polarity is not always applicable and yet people often apply it, without realizing so, as a way to understand and communicate, as well as to separate. Polarity and the more subtle Duality of Polarity is evident in some of the most primal universalities and is so elusively omnipresent that people often utilize it to communicate even without realizing so.

The Duality of Polarity is a way to understand scientific and political concepts, it's a window into the human condition, our very consciousness, and knowledge of it can instigate awareness of self and surroundings. The Matrix of Four begins with universal absolutes and through the matrix of itself, provides a base understanding of ourselves. The metaphilosophy is one way to critically examine the external universe as well as our internal space. It is not the only way, it is not the definitive way, but it is a highly effective way used for millennia, aimed at contrasts and not contradictions, aimed at unification, not separation.

Many systems contain obvious polarity and a corresponding subtler secondary duality of polarity. This knowledge can be employed to more sufficiently explain as well as more efficiently contemplate. One day has four parts; dawn, day, dusk, night. One year has four seasons; spring, summer, fall, winter. A day and a year might be understood in any number of ways and yet the simplest way to understand the totality of a day, and of a year, is through the Matrix of Four, The Philosophy of The Duality of Polarity.

Both orbit and arithmetic have basis in The Duality of Polarity despite the infinite structure of the universe and mathematics. The Matrix of Four, The Philosophy of The Duality of Polarity is based on the absolutes of orbit and arithmetic. It is a metaphilosophy applicable to numerous objects and subjects, inside and outside, and can be used as tool for contemplation of the similar qualities shared by the universal and individual, the macrocosm and microcosm. It is based on the most reliable absolutes there are, and yet by itself it is not an absolute and as a metaphilosophy that accepts that, one you can consider. Philosophies which tout absolutism become manifestos and should be approached with extreme caution, or avoided altogether, no matter the authority the deliverer.

Endless Knot   Salomon's Knot

Chapter 1

The Magic of Breath

The Matrix of Four, The Philosophy of The Duality of Polarity is embedded into some of the most notable symbolism in the world. The mutual symbolism shared by diverse peoples represents our interlinked conceptualism, our collective perspective on a mutually recognized dynamic. It's likely that no other idea is as important or as frequently a part of as much symbolism of import as is The Matrix of Four, The Philosophy of The Duality of Polarity. Perhaps the mutual ideas related to the Matrix of Four originated in the four seasons and four operations of arithmetic, and perhaps these are but reflections of the matrix too.

The definition of a matrix is not a caging control system, like in the film The Matrix. A matrix is a womb which gives birth unto itself, infinitely. In the film the control web was the matrix. The Matrix of Four, The Philosophy of The Duality of Polarity is born from absolutes and is reflected infinitely among humanity's symbolism.

The matrix in the film The Matrix is a web of control, of machine over man, whereas The Matrix of Four is a matrix of consciousness. Many of the ideas allegorically portrayed in the film are discussed in the Matrix of Four, it being metaphilosophy, but this is not specifically about the net or web of the world that increasingly resembles the film, but rather about how to develop one's consciousness into a sharp tool to cut through such control mechanisms. The Matrix of Four, The Philosophy of The Duality of Polarity instigates individual consciousness and heightens political awareness of reality as allegorically expressed in the film, The Matrix, when Neo wakes up.

The Matrix of Four explores the illusory control grid depicted in the film The Matrix, similar in tone to *1984* and akin to the ancient Socratic Allegory of the Cave to enhance consciousness. The Matrix of Four, The Philosophy of The Duality of Polarity is metaphilosophy and thusly explores the underlying concept of The Matrix, inspiration of individuation. The Matrix of Four is empowering, among systems which would rather individuals not be empowered. The Matrix of Four is based on developing consciousness, not locking it down, like the mechanized control grid depicted in the film The Matrix. The Matrix of Four, exactly like the film The Matrix, explores the righteous rebel archetype that Neo portrays, and like the freed slave from the Allegory of the Cave.

The endless knot is a matrix symbolic for polarity and the endless interaction of opposing forces giving birth to the unification of opposites. It is similar in design to Celtic knots, Solomon's knot, as well as several other design traditions from around the world including Islamic interlacing patterns.

The endless knot is one of the Eight Auspicious symbols celebrated in Buddhism, Hinduism and Jainism. The other seven are the conch shell (four different colored conches represent different societal castes), lotus flower (there are four, sometimes five different colored lotus flowers; white, red, blue and pink, each symbolic for differing stages of consciousness), the wheel, parasol, two golden fishes (symbolizing the polarity of male and female energies), victory banner (symbolic of victory over the Buddhist four hurdles to spiritual development; emotional defilement, passion, fear of death, pride and lust) and the treasure vase.

The endless knot is a metaphysical matrix, symbolic of the duality of polarity through the squares within squares and the unification of opposites infinitely. The endless knot symbolically portrays a metaphilosophical matrix in the design and the ideas behind the design. One of the narratives behind the endless knot is that it reflects the mutual dependence of spirituality and secularism, and of consciousness and science. The endless knot philosophically and visually depicts The Matrix of four.

Another highly regarded idea among the unification of opposites and contrasts presented in the endless knot is the union of wisdom and method or the union of wisdom and compassionate approach. One has to know before one takes action. One has to have the theory before attempting the practice. This is true in life as well as in art, whether the art is visual, or literary, or otherwise. One must obtain wisdom before compassionate action and before methodical action. Without wisdom there is no compassion and no artistically worthwhile method. All artistic endeavors as well as the art of life are not as extraordinary as they could be without development of wisdom and method. Many people live with improper wisdom and/or improper method their whole life, never seeking to better either their wisdom or method. Proper wisdom and proper method lead to quality art and compassionate being.

The most popular Buddhist mantra is Aum mani padme hum. It is the four symbol, six syllable mantra of Tibet, and Tibetan Buddhism. Said to be the mantra of Buddha, Aum mani padme hum is a matrix of four. Aum, most often spelled Om, and traditionally only drawn symbolically, depicts four states of consciousness and specifically in this mantra Aum symbolizes the universal macrocosm. Mani means jewel and stands for the jewel that is compassionate being. Within mani are the three jewels that are the Buddha, the (Buddhist teaching) Dharma and those around who understand the Dharma. Together they make the fourth jewel of integration called vajra. Padme means lotus flower (symbolized with four leaves) and in this mantra symbolizes method and contains four aspects, yantra, (philosophy) mantra, (sound) mudra, (physical positioning) and tantra (integration). Hum, like Aum, has three sounds plus silence and stands for the notion of please, as well as the microcosm and integration. Hum contains four and sometimes five parts; earth, air, water, fire (and ethereal) elements and represents the five awarenesses and the four foundations of mindfulness.

The Aum mani padme hum mantra of Tibet stands for universal compassionate wisdom and method applied to the macrocosm of surroundings through the microcosm of self. The endless knot and Aum mani padme hum are both matrixes of four reflecting the universal and individual through and into each other like metaphysical mirrors. Aum mani padme hum is said to be activated by a fifth part, shri or hri. These concepts and the Matrix of 4 within them point to development of compassionate being.

"Om is the infinite, but hum is the infinite in the finite, the eternal in the temporal, the timeless in the moment, the unconditioned in the conditioned, the formless as basis of all form, the transcendental in the ephemeral: it is the wisdom of the great mirror, which reflects the Void as much as the objects, and reveals the 'emptiness' in things as much as the things in the 'emptiness. To see things as parts, as incomplete elements, is a lower analytic knowledge. The Absolute is everywhere; it has to be seen and found everywhere." ~Lama Anagarika Govinda, Foundations of Tibetan Mysticism

Solomon's Knot, sometimes called the foundation knot or duplex knot, is depicted with four sides, often in varying shapes, circles, triangles and squares are used. Like the endless knot it reflects infinity and eternity. Little is known as to the specifics of Solomon's Knot though it certainly artistically illustrates the Matrix of Four, The Philosophy of The Duality of Polarity. It is obviously related to the Seal of Solomon, the same basic design as above utilizing opposing intertwined pyramids, a two dimensional depiction of the Merkaba, the legendary three dimensional metaphysical figure of intertwined opposing four sided pyramids or tetrahedrons.

Art is the combination of wisdom and method, as is living one's life. All artistic endeavors, including writing are meditative acts. Art transforms intangible thoughts into tangible communication, interlinking wisdom and method. Visual art can be as simple as intertwined linear shapes and still hold deep significance when the wisdom and method are proper. In writing, this is done through the symbolism of words. The wisdom is the philosophy, the method is the word. In living a happy life the wisdom and method is blossoming compassionate thinking and being as depicted in Aum mani padme hum, expressing the link between wisdom and method, macrocosm and the microcosm.

The Matrix of Four, The Philosophy of The Duality of Polarity provides understanding of the universe outside and the universe within. The idea explores relationships and presents a formula for contemplation and problem solving. The Matrix of Four is a metaphilosophy and as such it is equally spiritual and secular, equally meditative and political, applicable to universal and individual understandings alike.

"All know that the drop merges into the ocean, but few know that the ocean merges into the drop." ~Kabir

The formula of The Matrix of Four results from the unification of diverse ideas, utilized by ancient and assorted peoples, based on science and theology, intuition and reason. The Matrix of Four, The Philosophy of The Duality of Polarity assists in understanding complexities of universal systems, as well as individual and collective consciousness. Through the duality of polarity in the four seasons and four operations of arithmetic we gain understanding of, and tools for, multiple subjects and objects. And with the physical and spiritual absolutes we gain even more understandings and useful tools. The Matrix of Four results in heightened awareness of diverse systems and unification of the macro and micro, of wisdom and method. Meditation is perhaps the ultimate individual act unifying wisdom and method, while possibly political interaction is the ultimate collective act doing so.

One of the most powerful meditations is the Metta meditation from Buddhism. There are many meditations which contain the main aspects of the Metta, meaning loving kindness, for practicing such open compassion allows one to be more open to energy and experience. The Metta meditation begins by relaxing and then imagining compassion for self and others. Metta is based on the set of four universal wishes; peace, safety, happiness and love. First focus on love of self; may I be happy, may I be safe and at ease, may I be happy and may I be loved. In between each thought practice simply being present and breathing momentarily. Then imagine these same wishes for a friend or loved one, then someone in your life interaction, then someone who you are experiencing difficulty with, then the entire world.

There are countless specific forms of meditation, however there are just four basic physical positions for meditation. Angeles Arrien noted these four basic positions in her book The Four Fold Way; Walking the Paths of the Warrior, Teacher, Healer and Visionary. In it she uses indigenous correlations to describe four forms of positive mentality as well as their opposing negatives or shadows. She then relates the four physical forms of meditation with the four mentalities of the warrior, teacher, healer and visionary. The four physical forms of meditation are standing, laying, walking and sitting positions. There are four basic physical forms of meditation though there are thousands of specific practices, procedures and postures including yoga asanas and tai chi chuan forms.

"In a solitary place, like a forest, the yogi should practice all Four Actions, and balance the Four Inner Elements. Thus, the Wisdom of Four Blisses will in his mind appear." ~Milarepa

Long ago, yoga practitioners and meditators, like Milarepa, referred to these differing physical positions as the Four Actions. The Tibetan hero, magician and Saint Milarepa is the origination of the archetype of the wise meditator atop the mountain, and sang those words long after he had completed studying. To begin his studies though his teacher required him to build, what turns out to be, four houses before Milarepa was given instruction. The four houses are said to represent the four types of meditative actions or magical approaches. The first house Milarepa builds is a circle, representing peaceful action and water. His teacher rejects it. The second house is a crescent building representing powerful action and air. Again, it is rejected. The third house is a triangle house representing fascinating action and fire. The fourth house is square, representing stern action and earth.

Milarepa was known as a magician who became enlightened and in several of the stories about him and his songs, he explores what is arguably the duality of polarity of magic. This is depicted in the Challenge of the Logicians. Some visit Milarepa to question his knowledge of the dharma whereupon Milarepa changes the density of a rock so that it is like air and changes air so that it is like a rock. The duality of polarity of magic is changing our perception so that our perception can then cause change. We are accustomed to space being intangible and solids such as rocks being impenetrable. Magic flips this situation, magic is the solidification of space into density and the dispersal of solid into the airiness. Magic makes the obstructing non-obstructing, and vice versa, by, as Milarepa put it, the Samadhi (meditation) of solidifying space and Samadhi of space exhaustion. The story inspires questioning the nature and the density of our thinking and being.

In the same way there are four basic physical positions there are four basic mental positions for meditation as well, though again there are thousands of specific practices. Meditation is about clearing through the mind to connect with oneself. Other times it is about finding something outside oneself, perhaps a solution to a problem. We can direct meditation in four mental directions formed via the intersection of two applications of mindfulness/emptiness, and internal/external focus.

The first application is one of mental fullness or mental emptiness. Meditation with mental fullness crowds the mind with an idea. Meditation with mental emptiness clears the mind of all ideas so as to relax. The second application is of inward and outward concentration or reflection. One peers inward or outward with either a clear or crowded mind. Most meditation promotes a clear mind while peering inward. Many forms of Sufi meditation crowd the mind peering outward. One way to solve problems is in this way, imagining the dilemma and a solution. Albert Einstein famously would perform thought experiments crowding his mind with ideas in this way. Psychic meditation clears the mind while peering outward. Healing meditation practices might crowd the mind with an image of healing while peering outward or inward depending on the process. In some meditations the positions are variously alternating between crowding and clearing the mind.

Some forms of meditation are efficient at problem solving in the world while others are efficient at potentiating inward development or solving problems within ourselves. Yet whatever the specific variation practiced one either crowds the mind or clears the mind, while peering inwardly or outwardly. Relaxed awareness of the four physical and four mental positions of meditation, can hone and enhance one's meditative practices. The knowledge can also raise meditative mind state when you're performing your activities in daily life enhancing your conscious intent.

Relaxed awareness of intention is essential in all forms of meditation, whether seeking answers in thought experiments or Zen stillness, whether for external problem solving, or internal insight, or healing. Awareness of the four forms of one's physical and mental positioning enhances meditation. The most powerful meditation intention is to essentially become a conduit of goodness and through the flowing of goodness and compassion to others goodness flows through you and to you.

This idea of transmitting goodness goes beyond Buddhism, but Buddhism presents it perfectly and eloquently as foundational lessons and specific meditation techniques. Buddhism is based on the Four Thoughts, (we are precious, impermanent, formed by karma and bound the world of samsara-suffering) the Four Immeasurables (loving compassion for self, loving compassion for others love for the happiness of others and love for all things in equanimity) and the Four Noble Truths (truth of suffering, truth that root of suffering is craving, truth that cessation of suffering is cassation of craving, truth that the path to cessation is through the Eightfold Path of Enlightenment). The Four Thoughts, Four Immeasurables, Four Noble Truths, along with the Eightfold Path and Six Paramitas, are some of the most powerful meditation tools, and the most fundamental principles utilized in Buddhism. Equally important to conscious compassionate intention in meditation, according to diverse traditions, is the conscious and calm awareness of the breath, specifically the four parts of breath.

All meditation practices note that the awareness of the breath is primal and essential. And every breath you take, every breath of all life on Earth is based on an exchange, based on a contraction and relaxation in the form of The Matrix of Four, The Duality of Polarity. There are four parts to every breath. The main polarization is inhalation and exhalation. And as is typical of so many sets of four, in the form of the duality of polarity, often the main polarization is the only one noticed and counted. Many only notice this main polarization. There are four parts to every breath according to longstanding meditation traditions where awareness of breath is essential. The pause full and the pause empty are the second polarity of breath.

Meditative breathing requires awareness of the breath. And every breath, meditative or otherwise, is taken in the form of The Matrix of Four, The Duality of Polarity; inhalation, pause full, exhalation, pause empty. And no matter how brief the pauses are made to be, they still exist. Those who practice meditation are taught to be calmly aware of these four parts. Sometimes one or another part is accentuated and sometimes a more cyclical breath is utilized and the pauses are minimized. In order to slow the breath, spend more time in the pauses.

A ratio of around 4 to 1 seconds seems to be balanced for simple inhalations/exhalations to pauses, but the ratio is not important relative to firstly relaxed approach, and also balance. Try to breathe in and out for about eight seconds and then pause in and pause out for two seconds and then slow it down from there and find your own rhythm. The pause full should most frequently done at no more than 80 - 85% lung capacity and pause empty at near 0% capacity. The breath, the essential basis of all life, the beginning to all meditation, and all action, is itself based on the duality of polarity, a set of four exchanging contrasts of one. Breath is the expression of the physical absolute of the duality of polarity.

Breath is at the basis of every thought and action and the duality of polarity is at the basis of every breath. The microcosm of each breath reflects the macrocosm of the duality of polarity of equinoxes and solstices. Breath is the primary one of the four ways humans and all animals obtain energy, the other three being through water, food, and chi or prana through meditative movement.

Despite the innumerable meditation variations there are four aspects to all forms of meditative breath. Awareness, consciousness of breath is the first aspect. Slow breath is the second important aspect. Thirdly is breathing deeply, through the spine, from below the navel and ultimately so deep you imagine the breath coming through the feet. Lastly is steadiness of breath. This steadiness can fluctuate as to timing, but awareness of the four parts to the breath is a simple approach to balancing the steadiness of breath.

Among the vast variation of meditations there are four forms of meditative breath to move one's energy in one way or another as opposed to balanced breath, to balance one's energy. As one masters balanced breath one can enhance one's energy movement, according to chi gung breathing understanding.

There are four basic forms or patterns to the breath set, similar conceptually to the depiction of the Yin Yang mandala. Unlike balanced breathing these forms build and release energy in specific ways. There is the enhancement and lengthening of the pause full: breathe in/pause/breathe out for Yin energy. There is the enhancement of pause empty: breathe in/out/pause for Yang energy. The second pair of opposites is the insertion of a pause in between either the inhalation or exhalation to build movement of energy, breathe in/pause/continue breathing in/out for Yin, and lastly breathe in/out/pause/continue breathing out for Yang. Inhalation expansion and pauses enhance Yin, while exhalation expansion and pauses enhance Yin. Balanced smooth breathing is recommended though, but for calming enhance the inhalation, for instance.

Chi gung also illustrates four pathways of energy through our energy systems; small circle or microcosmic with one pair of pathways and big circle or macrocosmic, followed by the crossing of the small and the crossing of the big. Chi gung is some of the oldest and original forms of meditative movements and yet also one of the most integrated of perhaps any meditative movement.

In tai chi and chi gung meditations there are also two main aspects of each inhalation and each exhalation. Imagine firstly inhaling into your lower belly and secondly into your lungs, and exhale out of your lungs then lower belly. This natural breath is sometimes called Buddhist breathing, concentration on expanding the lower belly on inhalation and contraction on exhalation. Taoist reverse breathing is the opposite, contraction of the lower belly on inhalation and expansion on exhalation.

Other more specific techniques involving timing and positioning of the tongue and breathing through a particular nostril or other variations all have different purposes for building and releasing energy in different ways and are practically all designed to build the awareness of slow, steady, deep breath greatly assisting health and concentration. Generally one should keep your mouth shut and tongue on the roof of your mouth without tension in your mouth or jaw. Understanding the breath is required for the inner journey of meditation in the same way that understanding orbit and our spherical revolution is required before journeying out to sea and each can offer understandings greater than the original context and intent.

Quality meditative breathing requires a relaxed mind state. This state of relaxed awareness can be acquired in meditation and enhances meditation. In tai chi there are four primary martial energies; an -push, ji -press, lu –roll away and peng -ward off used to stay balanced under attack and four secondary energies. In tai chi practice there are also the four gates to open for higher flow and four cavities which hold potential energy.

The idea of balanced living and moving in tai chi and all meditative movements is best expressed using a cross reference of the Matrix of Four, The Philosophy of The Duality of Polarity. Consider one can be tense or limp and that relaxed awareness is balance between the two, the midpoint of a horizontal line. Consider also that one can perform actions out of form or function, optimally a balanced midpoint between the two points on a vertical line. Relaxed awareness is a requirement and conversely a result of meditation and meditative movement and can be represented as the point where these two ideas intersect and balance. This point of relaxed awareness is achieved when one properly intersects and balances the linear ideas of tense and limp, with form and function. Whenever performing any activity the proper state is required for optimal result, be it tai chi or meditation or anything.

"The loose string, which is like a life of indulgence, produces a poor sound when struck. The overly tight string, which is like a life of extreme asceticism similarly produces a poor sound when struck and is moreover likely to break at any moment. Only the middle string, which is like the middle path, produces a pleasant and harmonious sound when struck." ~Story of Buddha

Tai chi and similar meditative movements activate all aspects of self-awareness, physical awareness, and metaphysical or intuitive awareness. The first level of awareness is gained simply through being alive though it's multiplied through practice of meditative movement. It is called interoception, this is the understanding of the one's material self. Hunger and physical discomfort are stark examples of interoception. The second level of understanding is exteroception, the understanding of the material world outside oneself, other beings and the earth elements are examples. The third level of awareness is proprioception, the understanding of how much strength, speed, and from what position one can best manipulate or deal with the material world outside oneself. The fourth aspect of this set of four forms of awareness or perception is preprioception, the utilization of intuitive understanding and subtle sensitivity. Tai chi and all meditative movement enhance these four forms of perception, expanding one's perimeter awareness, physically and metaphysically. Interoception, exteroception and proprioception are commonly understood terms, but the fourth part, obvious to meditative movement practitioners, is mostly unconsidered and unmentioned.

The Aum sound and symbol is one of the oldest symbols in existence and in part is a representation of mind states, or levels of awareness. Aum originates in the Hindus Valley, the region to which the Vedic principles, Jainism and many other spiritual understandings have roots. Aum is used as a beginning point for prayers, mantras and/or meditations. It is used in combination with other sounds or by itself as part of meditative processes to reach that point of relaxed awareness. Aum can be seen as the ancient Sanskrit symbol for God, but it is more than that. It is said to be the sound and symbol of the creation of the cosmos. It is possibly the very oldest symbol on the planet, and it is at the basis of the oldest theologies, as well as being highly revered in Buddhism. The symbol is of a sound as well as a philosophy. Aum, like many ancient and powerful symbols, is directly and exactly reflective of The Duality of Polarity in its depiction, its vocalization, and its philosophy of consciousness.

The sound of Aum used at the beginning of mediations and mantras contains four parts. It is known as the unstruck sound, the sound that just is. There are A, U and M sounds in its pronunciation and the fourth sound, the unspoken aspect, is the sound of silence. Aum is A,U,M, and silence.

The symbol of Aum displays four main parts or states, in the four curves, the fourth and pinnacle state being behind the veil, symbolized as the point. The philosophy behind the four different parts of Aum relates the four different levels of consciousness beginning with the waking state and the dream state being the first two polarized parts. These are the two main polarizations of consciousness people generally go through on a day to day basis. The third state, the curve above the bottom two, is the deep sleep state, which is akin to being in a meditative state of relaxed awareness. And the fourth state, the most developed and distinct of this set of four, is deep awakening, known as the oneness behind the veil of illusion. It is the distinct one above the others, it is the supreme state which is difficult if not impossible to describe, let alone to attain. It is also known as the point of truth behind the veil.

Discovery of the set of four in Aum sent the biggest shivers of signification I experienced in researching this idea. I then concluded the idea was not a new idea I found, but an ancient idea that found me, and I was able to transmit anew.

The four states of Aum represent the four states of consciousness, the spiritual absolute, if you will, on which the Philosophy of The Duality of Polarity is based along with the natural, physical and mental absolutes. The presentation of these states of consciousness are not simply four in number, but they in the formation of The Duality of Polarity; the conscious, unconscious, subconscious and supreme consciousness. Deeper philosophy still recognizes three transitional stages in between each of the four stages equating seven stages, the four main parts, and three more subtle transitional parts.

The Hindu idea of Turiya relates to the four states symbolized in Aum. Turiya proposes that the first three states are parts of and lead up to the fourth part which is the supreme state of consciousness, of bliss. Most Turiya philosophy points to the fourth state as pinnacle though sometimes a fifth stage is equated to this development of consciousness. Turiya, Aum and the mantra Aum mani padme hum each contain aspects of the duality of polarity, and point out that the fourth part is the higher aspect and is made up of the first three parts.

The four parts to the visual depiction and vocalization of Aum and the philosophy of consciousness behind it, and that of Turiya are reflective of the Matrix of Four and matrixes on their own. Aum begins as a physically derived idea, as well as a godly one, with the notion that it represents the creation of the cosmos. And it expands inwardly, as a conceptualization of consciousness, while eluding on how to develop our consciousness. Aum is based on four parts and depicts the duality of polarity in its elaboration on human consciousness. An abstract correlation is that Aum, the unstruck sound, represents the unstruck all permeating forces of the universe, gravity as well as consciousness.

The sound has four parts and the fourth part is distinct and special among them; silence. The symbol has four parts to it; the wake state and sleep state and the second polarization of deep sleep and deep awakening. Deep awakening is the distinct fourth part of the set. It is Maya, depicted as the curve below the point, that requires piercing to get through, and some compare getting past it to crossing a sea.

The Upanishads, sacred Hindu writings, known to be influential on Ancient Greek philosophies as well as the thinking of other cultures, suggest that transcendence of the three states into the fourth state, piercing the veil of Maya, offers liberation. Maya is sometimes described as sea of

27

suffering. Aum depicts the transcendence and heightened awareness of the fourth part from unconsciousness to supreme consciousness. The Philosophy of The Duality of Polarity depicts the same; the development of four forms of consciousness. Throughout recorded time there have been four forms of consciousness however subdivided and however borne to countless different names and different sets.

The Hindu idea of measuring time in epochs of Yugas presents the metaphysical orbit of the universe, the entirety of creation in The Four Yugas. The Four Yugas comprise one of the grandest measurements of time, based on a revolution akin to our solar system resulting in four earthly seasons, only the Yugas are celestial seasons. In the Yuga orbit the entirety of creation revolves around the central metaphysical Sun, the Sun of truth of peace, just like the Earth revolves around the Sun. As we experience spring, summer, fall and winter on Earth, in the cyclical span of the Yugas we experience consciousness or reality as full truth, mostly truth, mostly deception and all lies and deception in a cycle composed of four seasons, each in the hundreds of thousands of years. We are said to currently be in the time of all lies and deception, known as the Kali Yuga.

Arthur Schopenhauer, a German philosopher born in 1788, called the Hindu Vedas, (made up of four basic parts; the Samhitas, Brahmanas, Aranyakas, Upanishads) 'a production of the highest human wisdom.' He was heavily influenced by Vedas, and Buddhism, and highly influential on Einstein, Tolstoy, Freud and Jung. Schopenhauer authored *On the Fourfold Root of the Principal of Sufficient Reason* in 1813 and revised it over thirty years later. This text describes four classes of human reasoning; becoming, knowing, being, and willing. The distinct and most developed part of this set, corresponding with the transcendence represented by the fourth part of Aum, is willing.

"Philosophy...is a science, and as such has no articles of faith; accordingly nothing in it can be assumed as existing except what is either positively given empirically, or demonstrated through indubitable conclusions." ~Arthur Schopenhauer

The Matrix of Four, The Philosophy of The Duality of Polarity is based on a number of indubitable conclusions. The revolution of celestial objects has four balanced points of coming and going, no matter the time or distance involved. Mathematics is much more than addition, subtraction, multiplication and division, and yet these functions are formed exactly in the Duality of Polarity and are the basis for all of mathematics. Aum represents much more than the concepts explainable through the Matrix of Four, but it forms its basis. The Duality of Polarity is perhaps the oldest set theory there is, expressed in numerous inarguable conclusions, and as all metaphilosophy should be, demonstrated and applicable repetitively.

The Duality of Polarity often results in two corresponding or matching polarizations, like the four forms of arithmetic and the four forms of consciousness represented by Aum. Abstractly there are five possible sets of four beginning with a set where all are similar; AAAA, AAAB, AABB, AABC, ABCD. No matter the set there is frequently the distinct part, like silence or supreme consciousness or willing, a part that reflects the infinite transcendence depicted behind the veil of Maya. Frequently, no matter which abstract formation is apparent at the core of a Matrix of Four, there is the distinction of the fourth part. Individually this archetype represents the righteous rebel, the archetype represented by the freed prisoner in The Allegory of the Cave. The fourth part is also metaphilosophically speaking a completion. It is nullisis, in honor of the unlimited alternative surpassing dialectic limitations, explained in depth later.

One of the most widely worshipped Hindu Gods, often depicted within the Aum symbol and largely associated with Aum, is Ganesh. Ganesh is the elephant-headed god with one tusk and four arms. The Aum Symbol can be configured to outline both Aum and an elephant. Ganesh is the god or saint of writers and artists. His worship can be traced back to at least 500 BC, with roots in earlier traditions. Ganesh is known as both the obstacle breaker and correspondingly, potentially, the obstacle maker. All Hindu gods represent the polarity of positive and negative potentials. And each archetype is paired with a vehicle which assists them. Ganesh is paired with a mouse.

Ganesh is depicted with the contrasting mouse at his feet as his vehicle and partner. The actual and symbolic polarities between these two animals are many beginning with their size. Ganesh and his mouse symbolically and energetically work together to breakdown any barrier or obstacle, whether through the bashing strength of an elephant or through the incessant gnawing of a rodent.

Ganesh is said to be the scribe of the Mahabharata. The Mahabharata is a history of the world as well as a philosophical and devotional saga about the Vedic four purposes of life; righteousness, prosperity, pleasure, and liberation. Vyasa, the god known for splitting the single holy text of the Veda into four parts so people could better understand, asked Ganesh if he could write the story of the Mahabharata without making any mistakes. Ganesh answered he could as long as Vyasa wouldn't stop telling his story until finished. Vyasa replied he could as long as Ganesh understood everything before writing it down. Ganesh agreed. During the recital the pen broke and Ganesh used his own tusk as a pen when the original one failed, figuratively putting himself into the Mahabharata.

The Mahabharata and the Vedas of Hinduism are some of the oldest theological texts and they, like many religions and philosophies, note that all is one, in the spiritual realm, beyond the veil of illusion, like The Veil of Maya in Aum. And yet here on this plane, on Earth, all is polarized, but not necessarily in a manner which separates, and often in a way that unifies.

Hindu stories are so old as to have many layers of meaning and have multiple variations. One such story tells of competition between Ganesh and his brother, Kartikeya. A dispute over who was the wiser arose. They decided to settle it by seeing who could travel around the world. Kartikeya embarked on a world tour on his vehicle, a fast peacock. Ganesh remained at home with his counterpart mouse and traveled the world inwardly through his learning of all things. And when Kartikeya returned Ganesh simply drew a circle around his parents, or around a globe of the Earth, depending on the version of the story. Despite variations in the telling of the story the fundamental lesson remains that the internal traverse is much more expansive than the external one. Ganesh traveled the internal world through mental and spiritual investigation, while Kartikeya circumnavigated the world externally through physical and natural investigation. Ganesh was pronounced the wiser by all.

In Yoga tradition it is said people have seven main chakras, major energy points. In older tantric traditions from India and Tibet four main energy points or wheels considered. The four and seven chakras correspond with Aum where there are the four main parts and three transitions. Seven is widely celebrated and in seven there is the four. Look at your four fingers, there are three spaces between them. In the seven chakra system there are the four base chakras are compared to the four wheels of a chariot, they are the crown and throat in the front and the heart and base in the back, often hinted at being related to Ezekiel's chariot in the Biblical alliteration. The base chakra, at the perineum below the navel, is associated with Ganesh. It's represented with four lotus petals on the outside of a circle, with a square inside the circle, and an upside down triangle within the square.

Outright polarity is ubiquitous and subtle forms of the duality of polarity are frequently parts of patterns not limited to Aum and The Vedas, the four chakras as chariot wheels, the base chakra, or Gods and their vehicles. More importantly the duality of polarity is not limited to Hinduism or the world's religions, but it is intrinsic. The duality of polarity is a fundamental in our thinking and being and yet it is often missed, mistaken, ignored and hidden, no matter its ubiquity.

The sacred theosophy and theology discussed as a way to explore the duality of polarity is valuable in more ways than elaborated, and all such wisdom is layered. But The Matrix of Four, The Philosophy of The Duality of Polarity within them makes them valuable in revealing the formula, the metaphilosophy. The applications for the metaphilosophy are many, including and perhaps especially, toward understanding our individual consciousness and understanding how others think.

The social and political understandings of the duality of polarity are presented and the psychological models are thoroughly explored as are related meditative methods, but being a matrix there are always more applications. The metaphilosophy can be used in an indeterminate number of ways. The exploration of the duality of polarity within sacred ideas, like those that makeup Aum and are presented via Ganesh, is meant only as revered respect. But the power of the duality of polarity is derived scientifically and mathematically as well as in celebrated spiritually, making it unique among philosophy, making it metaphilosophy.

The symbolism of Aum represents the creation of the infinite cosmos and ultimately relates inwardly to human consciousness. Aum and the duality of polarity correlate the physicality of creation and the mentality of individuals, God the creator with our own consciousness. Objects of creation are all subject to gravity, which results in an elliptical coming and going measurable in four points via the duality of polarity. Even light cannot escape gravity and theoretically and it would seem light is also subject to the gravity of consciousness as well. Aum and the duality of polarity are based on the creation of the universe, the similar vibration of gravity and consciousness.

The philosophy of the duality of polarity is based on physics, making it difficult to argue, and the frequency of it as a basis in theosophy and philosophy make it impossible to ignore. Knowledge of it correspondingly makes one's arguments and observations difficult to disavow. It builds nuanced understanding of subjects and objects. The duality of polarity is not based on symbolism, or theological abstracts, but is a constant in some of the oldest, most influential symbolism and theology of the world. The frequency of its occurrence depicts resonance in thinking and being across time and space, our unity. There are many ways to understand objects and subjects however the Philosophy of The Duality of Polarity is a constant and inarguable way to consider many things, especially how people think, especially about consciousness. If one doesn't find shivers of signification in the matrix one will at least be capable of more nuanced thought processes and observational skills.

The duality of polarity is a philosophy on thinking and being, based on the absolute of orbiting spheres resulting in two solstices and two equinoxes, and the certainty of the four operations of arithmetic. These two absolutes in and of themselves have likely led to a greater understanding of the world and universe than any other information or discovery. These absolutes alone are enough to understand the duality of polarity and note its potential applicability. However when contemplating how people think, it is important to understand longstanding thoughts. And the thoughts, whether Hindu theosophy or otherwise, reveal how people think, as well as ways to apply the duality of polarity, and how it has been applied before.

Sacred stories, symbolism, theology, like that of Aum and Ganesh, are important windows into the subject of thinking and should be considered valuable for at least that to even the most enthusiastic atheist. The duality of polarity is at the basis of understanding the universe through its reflection in the revolution of spheres and the basis of mathematics, and it is part of the basis of humanity being central in some of the most powerful symbolism and theology. The Matrix of Four, The Philosophy of The Duality of Polarity is spiritually as well as scientifically validated repeatedly as important in referencing how we think, and much more.

Philosophy is the study of wisdom, of specific formulas for thinking and being. It is possible to hone one's thinking and being with philosophy so long as said philosophy is flexible and not an ardent manifesto of touted social and political absolutes. Theology is the study of spiritual wisdom and can hone one's thinking as well. Theology is often philosophical and philosophy is often theological. Whether Hinduism or any other religion, there is value in theology beginning with deliberation of how people think as well as how to develop one's thinking. Theology describes how people are and more importantly describes how we can be. Martin Luther King Jr., Malcolm X, Gandhi, and millions of others have taken theosophy and applied it to real action toward positive social and political development.

Gandhi explicated and practiced his peaceful proactive political philosophy through his four pillars; nonviolence, locally based (agriculture) cotton industry, Hindu-Muslim (oppositional) unity and an end to the prejudiced untouchable class system. His understanding of nonviolent action was based on the fourfold set of nonviolence; respect, understanding, acceptance and appreciation. Gandhi's philosophy of nonviolent political empowerment expanded into the fourfold set that runs contrary to so many institutional operations but so sensible for individuals; justice for all creatures, self-rule, localization enhancement and finally nonviolent, patient, revolutionary action.

Gandhi and other similar peaceful individuals did not build religious institutions which represented the philosophy and theology they applied. They made attempts to better themselves and uplift other individuals around them. They promoted individuation. They assisted individuals and sought to expand the Golden Rule. Religion builds institutions, theology builds individuals.

Religions are made of external institutions while theology is based on the study of internal spirituality and individuation. Theology seeks understanding, which is often lost to the institutionalization of religions. Dogmatic and franchise traditionalism is scorned by all the prophets and wise of theology, but nonetheless religions predominantly seek to develop the external position of their membership and not the internal disposition of their membership. Religion is not theology. Religions predominantly, like Kartikeya, focus on external exploration, while theology is primarily focused, like Ganesh, on internal exploration. They are brothers, but not the same. The value of theology and spirituality, from Aum onward, is in the power to facilitate and instigate thinking and being, not increase notions of us and them, or elevate religious institutions.

Without theological and mythological teachings, philosophical and divine truths, humanity would be lacking tools for spiritual awakening. Religious theology is philosophical and mythological and like all fables, adages and legends they bring to light our consciousness. And no matter the specific myth, no matter the truth of the story, it can always be reflected inwardly, as a development of consciousness. All theology is beautiful for the philosophical and mythological individuation, relation of macro and micro ideas, while all religions can be repulsive for their mechanization of zealous mind states.

"What all the myths have to deal with is transformation of consciousness...The individual has to find the aspect of myth that has to do with the conduct of his life. There are a number of services that myths serve. The basic one is opening the world to the dimension of mystery...but then there comes the cosmological aspect of myth, seeing that mystery as manifest through all things...but then there's another function and that's the sociological one, validating and maintaining a certain society, that is the side of the thing that has taken over in our world...but then there's a fourth function of myth and this is the one that I think today everyone must try to relate to and that's the pedagogical function, how to live a human lifetime under any circumstances, myth can tell you that."

~Joseph Campbell, Interview, The Power of Myth

The four functions and layers of learning from myth; opening new dimensions of mystery, the cosmological, the sociological and the pedagogical, can be used to enhance understanding of myth and more. Theology, metaphilosophy, news stories and what have you can all be viewed through this frame enhancing understanding of the story and how the stories impact thinking and being.

The Matrix of Four, The Philosophy of The Duality of Polarity is based on the four primal absolutes, the universal/natural, mental/mathematical, physical and spiritual absolutes. Celestial bodies cross the skies in revolution in the form of the duality of polarity. The four operations of arithmetic are in the exact formation of the duality of polarity. The matrix of four, the duality of polarity is at the basis of every exchange of breath. And it is integral in Aum, one of the oldest symbols on Earth used to understand god, creation and consciousness. The Matrix of Four, The Philosophy of The Duality of Polarity is based on timeless universal/natural, mathematical/mental, physical and spiritual absolutes reflected in the four seasons and in our very breath. Ultimately it can be utilized toward understanding one of the greatest complexities on Earth; the inner world of human consciousness.

Chapter 2

The Riddle

"Signs and symbols rule the world, not rules or laws." ~Confucius

The influence of symbolism often goes unnoticed, as do many influences. When symbolism goes unnoticed it still has meaning, resonance and influence. Perhaps unnoticed and unexamined symbolism is even more influential and has more potential to rule. When symbolism is understood one can understand its influences and the ideas behind symbolism more clearly. When one is ignorant of symbolism one might be more easily captivated by it. Signs and symbols rule when they are unexamined and unrealized. When they are understood, signs and symbols, and the influences promoting them, do not rule.

Today we use symbols primarily to evoke mundane ideas normally having to do with rules or promoting sales. Ancient symbols dealt in correlation of spirituality and science, the esoteric and realistic with multiple layers, stories and philosophies behind them. The richest symbols are often exquisitely simple, as well as accurately depictive of multiple systems providing insight into what at first may seem unconnected. The Yin Yang is one such symbol, and like Aum it is directly exactly reflective of the Matrix of Four, The Philosophy of The Duality of Polarity.

In Chinese the Yin Yang is called the Tai Ji, meaning The Grand Ultimate, partly because it connects to and is pertinent among so many things, in so many ways, in the microcosm and macrocosm. The Tai Ji contains Yin Yang. Some philosophies behind some signs and symbols promote limited thinking in ways that would benefit those who would want to rule the world whereas others open the mind to enable rule of self. Determining which philosophies and ideas are truths and which are non-truths is a continuous matrix of riddles itself. Correlating mental, physical, natural and spiritual absolutes with modes of thinking and being is a qualifier for a potentially more truthful philosophy.

Symbols containing subtle elements of the duality of polarity are numerous and it is overtly contained in many of the more prominent symbols. Many people, no matter how often they have considered breathing often only consider inhalation and exhalation. The Yin Yang symbol is often only considered by way of its stark singular polarity, ignoring the subtler secondary polarity.

 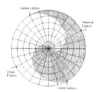

The philosophy behind the Yin Yang can open understanding, but misinterpretation of it can limit comprehension. The Yin Yang depicts the duality of polarity exactly and yet this overt aspect of the Yin Yang is often missed and mistaken for depiction of a singular polarity. The Yin Yang represents more than simply positive and negative or light and dark. The Yin Yang is the primal creative and receptive but it is made of the duality of polarity.

The Yin Yang represents the duality of polarity without one single veiling layer, despite the commonly accepted misinterpretation as being a singular polarity. The Yin (black) and Yang (white) swirls, each lead into the other, positive and negative, together in one circle or ball rather. The second polarity is in each part, there is the Yin in Yang, and the Yang in Yin. This is reflective of the universal concept of the duality of polarity, the positive in the negative and negative in the positive. These are called the potentials.

The Yin Yang is known to depict celestial orbit, shaped in balanced swirls of equinoxes and solstices. It depicts electrical and bioelectrical energy as well, the infinite coming and going of positive and negative unified in balanced oneness. Within the Yin Yang there are four parts; the negative, the positive, the positive within the negative, and the negative within the positive. Other traditions hold it is made up of a different set of four parts; the positive and its potential, the negative and its potential, the line in-between, and the circle encapsulating them.

Each part is enveloped by the other, leads into the other, balances the other, and contrasts the other. Polarizations of contrasts create potentials and movement, just as positive and negative components are required to harness and use electricity. The Yin Yang symbol is an example of countering balance and fluidity, not opposition. The energies are known to be co-arising. The Yin Yang creates potential and is not stagnant. The Yin Yang and its duality of polarity is a spiraling spherical potentiation. It is simple and primal, but the grand ultimate, and pinnacle as well.

"One day the farmer's only horse ran away. His neighbor heard of the bad news and comes over to commiserate. "I heard you lost your horse. That's bad luck."

"Maybe it is and maybe it isn't," the farmer replied.

The next day the farmer's horse returned, but it brought along a drove of wild horses it befriended.

The neighbor congratulated the farmer. "This is such good luck," he says. "Well, who knows," said the farmer, "Maybe it is and maybe it isn't."

The next day the farmer's son decided to ride one of the new wild horses to break it in. The son was thrown from the horse and broke his leg.

Of course, upon hearing the news, the neighbor came over to offer condolences. "This is such sad and bad news."

"Well, who knows," said the farmer. "Maybe it is and maybe it isn't. Who knows what is good and bad?"

On the following day soldiers came by commandeering an army. They took sons from most of the surrounding farms, but because the farmer's son had a broken leg, he could not go and was spared." ~ Taoist Tale of Farmer illustrative of Yin Yang

Yin represents the shade, dark, mystery, passive, feminine, gravitation, and cold. Yang represents brightness, sunlight, clarity, aggressive, masculine, radiation, and heat. Together they are complete and are one. In numerous meditation practices the combination of feminine and masculine forces, as conceptualized in Yin Yang leads to balanced energy, healing and intuition. In Tai Chi Chuan (meaning grand ultimate long form or long fist) one can find the Tai Ji reflected through each of the meditative movements.

The idea of The Tai Ji or Yin Yang reaches back thousands of years. One legend has it the idea itself is said to come from observing the movement of the sunlight and shadows in a mountain valley. The first variation of the Yin Yang symbol appears in China as early as 1000 BC. In many instances only the main polarity is noted. The smaller portions, the transitions or the potentials within, are normally ignored, missed or omitted. Yet singular polarity would be static and the Yin Yang is not static, the parts interact, birth each other, and potentiate the other.

The Grand Ultimate is used to understand celestial bodies as well as our own internal bodies. The Yin Yang is the basis to the structure of Chinese Traditional Medicine. In this system there are four body types, five counting neutral, that being well and balanced. Our physical body can be imbalanced in four manners; hot, cold, dry or damp.

Philosophically speaking when only yes or no, one or the other of two extremes is considered, there are always more options. When the either/or polarity is instituted, usually by those looking to rule, separation takes place and not unification. The Yin Yang does not represent mere polarity and separation of opposites. It represents the duality of polarity, four contrasts of oneness, unification of potentiation of co-arising opposites in movement.

There are the four visual parts of the Yin Yang and there are also traditionally four main aspects of the Yin Yang. It is made of related opposites. They are interdependent parts. They consume and support each other. They transform into each other.

The duality of polarity is demonstrable in the four parts and four aspects of the Yin Yang. One could make the case that the duality of polarity is derived from Yin Yang philosophy in the same way one could argue it is derived from the theosophy of Aum. However it is more accurate to say that truth correlates and great truth correlates profoundly. The duality of polarity is in each of these symbols, but within each of these symbols is much more.

The Yin Yang symbol has Chinese origins however similar designs were used throughout the world as powerful symbols regardless of the variances of specific meaning. Roman infantry emblazoned the symbol onto their shields as early as the fourth century and Celtic art from around the same time utilizes variations of the symbol as well. Some of these symbols contained just two swirls without the corresponding portions within, others contained numerous swirls.

The Yin Yang theory is said to represent the secret of the universe, the polarized balance of all things, the grand ultimate. It is an integral to classical Chinese science, philosophy, martial/meditative arts and medicine. It is representative of the complimentary relationships of related opposites, the universal balance.

The tenth century Song Dynasty philosopher Zhou Dunyi wrote The Explanation of the Diagram of the Supreme Ultimate exploring the concept of the Yin Yang or the Taijitu. The first sentence in the book suggests the meaning of Yin Yang and perhaps initiated its riddle.

"The supreme polarity that is non-polar." ~Zhou Dunyi, Explanation of the Diagram of the Supreme Ultimate

Opposites exist in relation to each other and even contain elements of each other. They do not exist in separation. The secret to the riddle of the Yin Yang is the duality of polarity. It is polarization with integration. Polarization without integration is mere black and white thinking. Polarization with integration, as represented in the Yin Yang, leads to understanding of the parts of the whole, the oneness. In the Yin Yang symbol four related contrasts are displayed and yet are often mistaken for two oppositions.

The supreme polarity is non-polar because ultimately all is one. It is a form of unification, as represented by the circle enclosing the Yin Yang itself. The duality of polarity does not create opposition, but allows complete understanding of contrasts and relationships. Parts are polarized, but because of their intimacy they are also interdependent and integrative. The Yin Yang symbolizes the idea of the great polarization of the contrasting balance of entirety.

Four, through the duality of polarity, is symbolic for completion. It is based on a prime and ultimate rule that balance necessitates polarity. The movement of celestial orbs is ruled by the duality of polarity. All mathematics is based on four operations of arithmetic shaped by the duality of polarity. We breathe by way of its format for a lifetime. The main philosophy of Aum and many primal parts of most Hinduism are based on it. And the main philosophy of the Taoists behind the most well-known symbol from ancient China is based on the duality of polarity too. Both Aum and the Tai Ji or Taijitu are celebrated as the grand ultimate and both exactly depict the duality of polarity, despite being unsaid or overlooked behind their overall greatness.

The duality of polarity is expressed in the tangible and the intangible, in physical practice and philosophy theory. The duality of polarity does not separate, but observes entirety like the Ying Yang, how things contrast and change, how one part flows into another, how there is positive and negative and how there is positive in negative and negative in positive.

"The unlike is joined together, and from differences results the most beautiful harmony."
~Heraclitus

Part of the secret to the riddle of the Yin Yang is also part of the secret of the duality of polarity. Each offers a way to understand all information, hence the grand ultimate idea. We are perhaps physically caught up in and depict the duality of polarity. Physically, for practically any movement there is basically four ways to vary it. Not so abstractly we can move our hands and bodies in four basic ways and then in multiple variations of course. Picture spinning a stick one way with one hand then the other way with the same hand, the same is possible with the other hand. This principle is noted throughout the martial arts, yoga movements, as well as any activity, snowboarding and skiing for instance.

There are also four types of information. This primary set of the matrix of four repeats and varies and is formed through the intersection of known and unknown. This presentation of the singular polarity of known and unknown is too simple to be complete, not enough to understand totality, just as understanding the Yin Yang as two parts is incomplete. To be complete the duality of polarity must be implemented as demonstrated by the same cross referencing involved within the energies at play within the Yin Yang and the same transformational potential. There are four types of information; the known knowns and the unknown unknowns are the two main portions. There are also the two minor parts; the known unknowns and the unknown knowns.

There are things we know that we know. There are things we know that we don't know. There are things we don't know that we don't know. And there are things we don't know that we know. These are the unknown knowns. The unknown knowns are the most complicated and distinct part to the set. These are the most difficult part to articulate, like the fourth part of Aum. The unknown knowns include secrets held by others and dichotomously, secrets –intuitive and instinctual capabilities for example, held by self. Within oneself unknown knowns can be valuable intuitive insight or burdening instinctual reactions one is unaware of. Secrets that others know and you do not know can be classified as unknown knowns too. Just as there are four parts of the Yin and Yang, there are four types of information. And just the same they each have a transformative potential.

Recently a highly institutionalized individual related a portion of this primal duality of polarity and even wrote a book with the more obvious polarity as the title. And as typical for such institutional representatives he conveniently removed the distinct fourth part. The distinct one of the four was left out so as to remove from consideration that there are unknown knowns, secrets some know and others do not and because, philosophically speaking, it represents the unlimited alternative, including specifically, alternative to authority. Like all institutionalized individuals of his ilk, he would rather omit the fourth part from consideration for institutional purposes, as the fourth part leads to a more thorough investigation of objects and subjects, including institutions in control and their secrets.

"Now what is the message there? The message is that there are known knowns. There are things that we know that we know. There are known unknowns. That is to say there are things we now know that we don't know. But there are also unknown unknowns, there are things we do not know we don't know. So when we do the best we can and we pull all this information together, we then say well that's basically what we see as the situation. That is really only the known knowns and the known unknowns. And each year we discover a few more of those unknown unknowns. And it sounds like a riddle." ~Donald Rumsfeld

It sounds like a riddle, because it is a riddle. It's the riddle of the supreme ultimate, the Yin Yang, of the matrix of four, the philosophy of the duality of polarity. And it is all too typical that the fourth part of this primal duality of polarity gets omitted by institutions and institutionalized individuals seeking to control. The fourth part Donald conveniently removed, as have so many institutionalized individuals before him, is the unknown knowns. The formula noting the existence of the fourth part is simple enough and yet this fourth part is potentially complicated and often enough, it's avoided completely. The unknown knowns are intuition and instincts, but also describe secrets, information few know and many do not know and do not know others know. Ironically Donald's poetic reflection was an answer about war and chemical weapons in Iraq. To this day people are still trying to understand who knew what and when as it concerns the specific reasons for omission and addition of information prior the invasion of Iraq. And each year we discover a few more of those unknown knowns.

In the exact same way that the rotation of spheres results in pairs of equinoxes and solstices and in the same way that the Yin Yang forms pairs of opposites, there are four types of information. There are many moments in a year, but all occur during four seasons. Information is near infinite, but all of it can be understood as being composed of one of these four cardinal forms. The duality of polarity can be applied to explore information more thoroughly as well as the perspective of the provider of the information more simply.

"Simplicity is the ultimate sophistication." ~Leonardo da Vinci

Less than four is frequently insufficient and more than four is often unnecessary to form a complete understanding of a given subject or object, like the totality of information, of knowns and unknowns. Through the duality of polarity four is often the minimal amount needed to cover all the bases. Information on objects and subjects can be broken down using contrasting denominators like information is broken down via the intersection of knowns and unknowns. In this way the matrix of four, the philosophy of the duality of polarity provides base understanding for a multitude of objects and subjects.

The notion of Occam's Razor reflects this concept displayed in the duality of polarity of information. Occam stated: "Plurality should not be posited without necessity." Most scientists, artists and philosophers recognize the validity and value of simplicity and William of Occam's theory known as Occam's Razor. The idea underlines that simple is better, but only when suffice. There are infinite objects and subjects, concrete and abstract and all can be categorized and understood as one of four types of information. Such simplification toward understanding the whole through the matrix of four and the duality of polarity makes the number four Occam's most frequently used tool.

"Everything should be as simple as possible, but not simpler." ~Albert Einstein

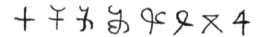

Development of 4

4 itself developed from a simple cross, two intersecting lines and eventually one part was made distinct. Now the number 4 appears as if a blade with a handle, ready to shave away the superfluous of any hypothesis, just as Occam and Einstein proposed. With the number 4, the simple totality of situations may be better understood and then further examined. 4 is just enough and not too much to reach completeness. Through the duality of polarity, 4 is symbolically Occam's razor.

Mandalas are devotional art symbols from Asia. Many mandalas contain corresponding ideas with the Yin Yang only in much more complex variations. Hindu and Buddhist cultures utilize the art form in which the duality of polarity is centric. The word Mandala simply means circle, symbolic for oneness, yet the intricacy of the designs are anything but simple circles. The designs are most always based on four. Four is the cardinal number in this spiritual art form and symbolizes, among many things, the four cardinal directions, the four gates of heaven and four gates of consciousness. The central circles in the designs are normally four layered representing philosophical levels and states, some in correspondence with Aum, for meditative purposes. In most all Mandalas four gates are depicted and then the four points in between and the center point. Carl Jung noted that Mandalas and similar designs were reflective of the individual awareness of a collective consciousness resulting in similar designs in different times and places.

The duality of polarity makes four special as exemplified in the four types of information in the known/unknown intersection and as symbolized in being the preferable razor of Occam. The matrix of four works through contrast of ideas and examination of the in-betweens as represented in mandalas. The four parts of the Yin Yang symbolize oneness and at the same time illustrates two pairs of polarizations. The Yin Yang and the duality of polarity do not divide, but contrast and simplify, like Occam's razor. Mandalas do not note separation, but the relationships of in-betweens, the interrelationships. The four cardinal directions assist in understanding location and direction while the duality of polarity forms four cardinal points of a given object or subject for reference, such as the intersection of knowns and unknowns.

Measurements of length, depth, width and velocity of a river work with each other to summarize the river. The measurements contrast in order to understand the river not to separate the ideas of it. They are not divided, but combine to reach understanding. Thinking in terms of this or that, considering only one side of the river or the other is limited and limiting and does not apply critical thinking to its entirety.

The Yin and Yang represents the duality of polarity, the great pole, not just one or the other, not just opposites, but flowing integration and balance. Four parts to a set is symbolic of balance and the minimum number required for completion, just as a table would be off balance and useless with two or three legs, and more than four legs is unnecessary. Four represents balanced completion.

All is one. And yet one must figuratively excavate underneath an object or subject and assess its basis to understand it. The duality of polarity is an efficient tool for excavation, for clearing the superfluous toward understanding the basis of objects and subjects. The matrix of four, the philosophy of the duality of polarity is not the answer to everything, but is the answer to the riddle of the great ultimate pole.

"As the Great Ultimate becomes differentiated, the two modes (Yin Yang) appear. Yang descends and interacts with Yin, and Yin rises to interact with Yang, and consequently the four forms (major and minor Yin and Yang) are constituted. Yin and Yang interact and generate the four forms of heaven: the element of weakness and the element of strength interact and generate the four forms of Earth; and consequently the eight elements (heaven, water, fire, thunder, wind, water in motion, mountain and earth) are completed. The eight elements intermingle and generate the myriad things."

~ Shao Yong, Song Dynasty philosopher

"Any fool can make things bigger, more complex, and more violent. It takes a touch of genius and a lot of courage to move in the opposite direction." ~Albert Einstein

Chapter 3

The Cross

It is impossible to know how influential the knowledge of equinoxes and solstices has been throughout history, as people seasonally migrated, seasonally harvested and erected structures which celebrate the seasons. It is also impossible to say what discoveries this knowledge might lead to as it is used to seek the slight wobbles of distant stars in search of other planets in the vast universe.

It is equally impossible to know the totality of the theological relationships of world religions. That which we do know however leads to the conclusion that all theology is more interrelated than most would like to admit. Religious dogma is often divisive. The history of religion however leads to the insight that our interpretations of God are either directly related or indirectly related through mutual natural observations, such as observing the equinoxes and solstices.

The history of the world's major religions is a series of adopted and transformed ideas. The religious tales of the Nubian, Egyptian and Babylonian cultures were adopted and used in the Old Testament millennia ago. The Old Testament transformed into the New Testament and later the Koran developed off of that. The world's three major religions; Judaism, Christianity and Islam, are closely related. They all have stories involving some of the same people. And yet today their followers are frequently ardently divided even though all three seem to be worshipping the same God, albeit by different names. Through the Matrix of Four, The Philosophy of The Duality of Polarity stark similarities can be noted in the theology of the three major monotheistic religions as well as the theology of other distinct peoples.

The story of the birth of Jesus, influential to so many, in so many ways, at least partly correlates with the crossing of the sun in the skies. The date of the celebration of his birth occurs during the winter solstice when the days are shortest and when they begin to lengthen. Pope Julius I set Jesus Christ's birthday on the winter solstice around 354 AD. He did so to attract pagans who celebrated the seasonal solstices and equinoxes. Easter, the holiday which celebrates the resurrection of Jesus, also correlates with the celestial event of the spring equinox in the northern hemisphere.

The cross is another symbol with as much power and sway in the world as the Ying Yang, Om, or any mandala, if not more. Variations of the cross symbol have been used for thousands of years across all four corners of the globe often symbolizing the four seasons. The cross is now commonly associated with Jesus and Christianity however it is an ancient symbol of the four cardinal directions and the four seasons that precedes Christianity's adoption of the symbol. Before the crucifixion of Jesus Christ it was a sign of crucifixion and punishment where such took place. Elsewhere it had much different meaning.

Native American cultures often displayed the cross in a circle, making four distinct parts within one. American Indians celebrated the cross within a circle and frequently used it as a trail marker of sorts in petroglyphs and in other sacred art. Variations of the cross within a circle are often called an American Indian medicine wheels, and like Asian Mandalas, they have spiritual and ritual significance. These medicine wheels, represent the elements as well as elemental philosophy and predominantly have four parts, and sometimes many more parts. Some depictions of medicine wheels are quartered into four different colors; red, yellow, white and black. Many Asian mandalas frequently utilize a similar color scheme however neither are limited to this color combination. Both Asian mandalas and American medicine wheels are predominantly based on four parts, through utilization of the cross, but sometimes are much more complex.

In ancient Celtic lands the cross was symbolic of the four seasons and great celebration occurred on the equinoxes and solstices as well as the midpoint between each solstice and equinox. The Celtic cross depicts these celebrations as does the Celtic double cross or eight pointed star.

Whether the cross is displayed within a circle or without a circle, all variations symbolize the idea of the matrix of four, the duality of polarity. Two intersecting lines create four points and four parts. This is a mathematical certainty, just like two plus two equals four. The cross represents the matrix of four and the duality of polarity. Two lines intersect and make four parts and two ideas intersect and make four points in the same way. Every cross and every mathematical illustration of two lines or two planes intersecting is directly illustrative of the duality of polarity.

Above is the Egyptian Ankh, followed by the Celtic wheel of life (similar to the depiction of the Buddhist wheel of life) and thirdly the Christian Cross. The cross symbol is celebrated independently among cultures across the world. The reverence of the cross is multicultural and though many of the ideas and philosophies behind the crosses are different, the reverence is the same. The philosophical specifics vary like the many variations in depiction, yet the matrix of four is always depicted in two crossing lines.

Four is embedded into the ancient philosophies and creation stories of many Native American peoples, perhaps none so significantly and extensively as the Hopi, Navajo and Zuni peoples of the Southwest. They celebrate four symbolically and philosophically in the symbol of the four quartered cross within a circle as well as other similar designs. Perhaps most significantly the Hopi believe we are living in the fourth world. Hopi tradition states the first world was Endless Space, the second was Dark Midnight, the third was the age animals and the fourth is the World Complete. Four migrations were written upon four sacred tablets which man was supposed to undertake migrations to share. Thousands of miles away and centuries before the establishment of the Hopi and Navajo the Mayan creation story, the Popol Vuh told of four gods and four first men.

An elaborate variation of the cross, the swastika, was used throughout the world for thousands of years before the Nazis adopted it. It was used by American Indians from Saskatchewan to Central America. The Kuna people of Panama believe the swastika shape represents the octopus that created the world in all four directions. The Swastika was used by the ancient Greeks to represent movement in art as early as the eighth century BC. The Hindus used it for thousands of years and it is still a holy symbol in Hinduism, Jainism, and Buddhism. Jain temples and texts must contain a swastika and it is essential to begin Jain ceremonies. The Sanskrit word swastika means auspicious object and it is often displayed with four dots at the four angled arms. It is representative of totality. And like all crosses it is also representative the matrix of four and the duality of polarity.

The Ancient Egyptian cross is the Ankh. It is one of the oldest and most distinguished crosses. The top section is not a line, but an oval. The mysterious symbol is said to represent eternal life. Hieroglyphs show Egyptian gods carrying one or a pair of ankhs and various sarcophaguses depict buried royalty holding ankhs. The ankh symbol was later adopted by Coptic Christians. The ankh has four parts, two matching lines, one longer line and a wholly distinct fourth part, the oval.

Blatant examples of the cross are used in many theologies, not just Christianity. However correspondingly and more significantly, the matrix of four the philosophy of the duality of polarity are presented in the beginning of practically every creation story, whether the Popol Vuh or Genesis. Nearly all creation stories start with the polarity of heaven and Earth followed by the polarity of male and female, the matrix of four, the philosophy of the duality of polarity. In this respect the matrix of four and the duality of polarity are at the basis of most all creation stories as well as being depicted in every cross.

In Genesis, the first story in The Bible, the polarities of heaven and Earth are immediately described followed by the polarity of male and female. Then the first four characters are described. These first four characters set the tone for the rest of the story. The first two characters are God and Adam. The next character is Eve, the feminine as opposed to the masculine and the fourth character is the serpent, the deceiver as opposed to the creator.

Nearly every theology, and philosophy for that matter, all point out the matrix of four, and its potentiation, whether subtly or not so subtly. The matrix of four potentiation results from the divine contrasted with the demonic, and our elemental physicality in respect to our elaborate spirituality. We choose. All people are capable of being as gods or being as dogs. This idea is in Christianity and nearly all theology, with varying interpretations.

"From a deeper point of view Yamantaka (in reference to a statue of The Slayer of Death, from Buddhist legend) represents the double nature of man, who shares his physical nature, his instincts, drives, and passions with the animals, and his spiritual nature with the divine forces of the universe. As a physical being he is mortal, as a spiritual being he is immortal. If his intellect is combined with his animal nature, demonic forces are born, while the intellect guided by his spiritual nature produces divine qualities." ~From The Way of The White Clouds, By Lama Anagarika Govinda

The matrix of four, the duality of polarity begins the Biblical creation story and is in the very symbol of Christianity, but there are other connections. There are four gospels in the Bible; that of Mathew, John, Luke and Mark. The Hebrew word for God is a four letter word, YHWH, known as the Tetragrammaton. The Tetragrammaton literally means four grammar, or language of four.

The four letters of YHWH are said to be symbolic of the Four Worlds of the Kabala; Emanation, Creation, Formation, and Action. The Four Worlds are spiritual layers of reality, though it's said that the final layer, Action, is both spiritual and physical. The Four Worlds are said to allow humanity to penetrate God Consciousness and understand creation of the cosmic and atomic, the self and surroundings. The understanding of the Four Worlds basically proposes that everything is composed of, and found in the Four Worlds, including the individual spirit.

Four is central to the celebration of Passover in the four questions, four cups of wine and four expressions of redemption. One could go on about the number of occurrences of four in the Old and New Testaments, but its representation in the Christian cross, its presence in the creation story and its basis in the Four Worlds of the Kabala, are alone reflective of its unique presence and major significance.

The universality of the cross and the matrix of four, the philosophy of the duality of polarity in Hindu, Taoist, Native American, Egyptian, Celtic and Judeo-Christian theology and symbolism illustrates its archetypal noteworthiness and the commonality of man. There are more instances of theological correlations with the matrix of four, and they all point to its noteworthiness as well as hint at different ways to utilize the metaphilosophy.

Jesus, Moses and dozens of other figures from the scripture appear in the Quran. The Quran means the recitation. Incidentally the Biblical Moses had four excuses or four expressions of self-doubt, in duality of polarity, when god asked him to be his messenger. Who am I to do this? Who are you to inform me of this? They will not believe me. I cannot speak well. But God convinced Moses to go forth anyway.

Islam means submission and obedience, and a Muslim is one who has submitted. The Quran describes believers and unbelievers as well as peacemakers and mischief-makers. The matrix of four and the duality of polarity of potentiation in the Quran is exemplified in the notion of believers and unbelievers cross referenced with peacemakers and mischief-makers. These four characterizations are frequently noted in the Quran and arguably form its basis of characterization.

All religious and philosophical texts might be interpreted differently by one or another and some believe there is no interpretation at all to holy books, that there is only one truth, usually their own. A critical divergence in the interpretation of theology is literal or allegorical. This is generally followed by questioning if the story is reflective of internal spirituality or external physicality. For instance, Islamic tradition holds that there are believers and unbelievers, peacemakers and mischief-makers in the external world, however some, a very few from what I understand, hold it is possible that this is, at least in part, reflective of the internal state of consciousness, our thinking as well as the resulting external being.

According to The Zohar, a Kabalistic text first publicly known in the 13th century, there are four ways to interpret theology and this understanding leads to ascension and paradise. Ascension is like shedding the cocoon of unconscious ignorance or so as to develop the butterfly of consciousness. Ascension of self and the collective consciousness begins with breaking patterns which unknowingly cause unhappiness, only then could we begin healing the destruction of global war and pollution.

The theological interpretive formula in the formation of the matrix of four is called the four PaRDeS. Legend has it understanding this formation of four is a final step on the path to scension. The capitalized letters represent the four aspects translated from Hebrew, in such translations vowels are ignored. Conveniently the combination of PRDS is similar to paradise, where ascension through consideration of the four aspects is said to lead. It is said, as one of the final steps to ascension, the knowledge can be dangerous, someone unready for the enlightenment of the four PaRDeS might be harmed in the same way a vessel unready for intense heat might be cracked. The most meaningful sets of four frequently contain this powerful attribute. And all enlightenment can shake, rattle and roll for most do not like change, even if it is ascension, even if their refusal to change pains them and holds them down.

The Four PaRDeS, the four forms of theological interpretation are the literal, allegorical, comparative and secretive perspectives. The first two are obvious, the comparative and secretive are more subtle and normally left unconsidered possibly because of the difficulty in deciphering such. Awareness of the four PaRDeS is valuable in understanding theological presentation as well as in understanding society.

The Four PaRDeS of theology extrapolated as a lens to view society can be layered firstly by surface understanding, our individual senses. The secondary more elaborate layer of understanding society arrives in the teachings of others. Thirdly is a combination of collective learning and our own experience used comparatively. Lastly is the intuitive approach where one cannot explain exactly how one reaches an answer, but the answer is nonetheless a useful one. Awareness of the four PaRDeS of interpretation is valuable in understanding theology as well as reality in society and can enhance intuitive understanding in total.

Sufism has ties to Muslim theology and many of its teachings are applicable to understandings of both our internal and external positioning. Some Sufism is devoted to the teachings of the Quran only, while other forms embrace different doctrines in universalism. Some say Sufism is an innovation extending from Islam while others say it predates Islam and all other religions altogether. Sufism notes polarity in practically all things and that any glimpse of oneness is the vector of all theology, the wine of the grapes that should be cherished.

There are countless powerful Sufi parables, tales and notions. One Sufi proverb puts forth the idea of the four gates of speech. Before speaking it is said one should pass one's thoughts through these four gates of examination:

Are these words true?

Are they necessary?

Are they beneficial?

Are they kind?

Of all theology the matrix of four, the philosophy of the duality of polarity is perhaps most starkly evident in the tenets of Buddhism. Buddhism is entirely based on The Four Noble Truths; the noble truth that suffering exists, suffering arises from desire, cessation of suffering comes through cessation of desire and the noble truth of the path to cessation of suffering is attained through the eightfold path to enlightenment. The Four Immeasurables and Four Thoughts also form its base. (See page 16) A Buddha is said to have four bodies; wisdom body, complete enjoyment body, emanation body and nature body.

In Buddhism there are four right exertions; restraint and abandonment of ignorance and evil, arising and maintenance of knowledge and good. The duality of polarity is not so subtly represented in the idea of restraint/abandonment and cultivation/preservation in the four right exertions. These ideas contrast one another and this is one of the most important sets of four, the consideration of which can lead to higher self-development.

The Buddha became aware of his path after what are known as the four sights on leaving his palace four times. The first three are sickness, old age and death. The fourth sight is the compassionate assistance of a monk. Prince Siddhartha seeks to be like the fourth from then on. There are four bases of power, four stages of enlightenment, and four great elements. The matrix of four and the duality of polarity are intrinsic in Buddhism and its overall presentation of oneness. Interestingly there is often noted to be three principle aspects of Buddhism; the principles (dharma), the enlightened one (Buddha) and the Buddhist community (sangha). But just like Aum there is a fourth part made up of the prior three parts, but distinct from them. The three aspects form the three sided diamond scepter jewel (Vajra) which like a diamond is clear, but reflects any color or subject of the prior three. The jewel is considered to lead to liberation and correlates with the heart and the diamond scepter our vertical consciousness. There are still the three universal truths in Buddhism; nothing is lost, everything changes and there is cause and effect to everything. The matrix of four is centrally important at the base of Buddhism and subjects beyond Buddhism, but it is not absolutely central to every aspect, always.

The matrix of four, the philosophy of the duality of polarity is symbolic for a complete basis as displayed via the ubiquitous notion of the primal four elements; Earth, water, fire and air. There are many more different elements however four provides a basic set of interpretation for them all. The cross inside a circle can be symbolic for the four quarters of Earth, the four seasons, four directions, and four elements. Crosses celebrate the matrix of four and the duality of polarity as well as perhaps symbolizing the human celebration of the basic four traditions; the four corners (quarters) of the Earth, the four seasons, four directions and four elements. There are of course many different elements and directions, seasons vary and there are no real corners on the globe, however they are celebrated regardless.

Various cultures in what is now China noted five base elements concerning certain systems and four elements among others and other ideas include the fifth element as the ethereal. Within all philosophy and theology other quantities are present and perhaps are as, or more integral than four. There are many other important systems which are not based on the matrix of four. One need not omit other quantities or systems solely to conceptualize four or utilize the duality of polarity. There are other numbers and other thought processes in which the matrix of four is not applicable. Yet that does not disregard the matrix of four, just to say there is no reason to project it or apply it where is doesn't belong.

The fact that four is venerated and symbolic for stable base completion and understanding across the cultural globe is undeniable. The matrix of four, the duality of polarity is not a theory to everything and it is not represented in everything, but it is applicable to many objects and subjects as a way to better understand them. And it is intrinsic in so many of the most important objects and subjects as to be ever present when other systems are in place like orbit and electromagnetism, breath and arithmetic. Some things are not necessarily interpretable through the matrix of four. One does not need to apply it to all things, like temperature or density or systems based on degrees or every single apparent trinity that suggests a missing elusive fourth part. Just being aware of the matrix, that it is occasionally intrinsic to systems and can be used to understand how people think can heighten one's own consciousness. By just being aware of the window one can better view object and subject, the macro and micro.

The fact that four is symbolic for completion is due to the equation of the duality of polarity; two intersecting lines make four points and in the same way two intersecting ideas make four points. Sometimes things are polarized many times, infinitely like in the endless knot. And sometimes objects and subjects work in layers having little to do with the matrix of four. Sometimes the matrix of four, the philosophy of the duality of polarity is not intrinsic. And yet it so often an applicable metaphilosophy concerning so many subjects and objects as to be exceptionally valuable, especially toward understanding and enhancing our thinking and being, our consciousness.

People traditionally note that we have five senses, while others count more like twenty, including the senses of pain, pressure, temperature, dilation and balance for instance, while others note even more, such as those related to precognition. The metaphilosophy of the matrix of four is a useful tool toward understanding and even towards enhancement of precognitive senses, but one does not have to omit obvious factors or sets to utilize it. The correct answer is not always four, but the matrix of four can practically always assist in finding the correct answer.

The matrix of four, the philosophy of the duality of polarity is valuable in exploring objects and subjects in part through knowing if and when it is applicable in the first place. Utilization of the philosophy of the duality of polarity does not require an obsession with four. People tend to polarize objects and subjects without realizing they are doing so. And in the same way people tend to project ideas, often without realizing so. Accurate utilization of the philosophy of the duality of polarity can assist examination toward understanding of objects and subjects, and most importantly can assist understanding the thinking and being of individuals and collectives, consciousness, through reflection. Projection is unnecessary and through understanding the concept becomes less likely.

The matrix of four, the philosophy of the duality of polarity is so frequently embedded into the symbolism, philosophy and theology of distinct cultures far and wide as to be recognizable as one way people think no matter where we're from, as part of our mutuality. It is possible to utilize the duality of polarity in both observation of the external world and more importantly in understanding how people think through cross referencing contrasts. And though other quantities are important and other numbers have inherent symbolic value, two intersecting lines, fields or concepts always equate to four points and then expand from there.

Chapter 4

From Egyptian to Jungian

The matrix of four, the philosophy of duality of polarity is useful in understanding natural conditions of the inner and outer world, both the esoteric and exoteric, the microcosmic and macrocosmic. As a metaphilosophy the models of intersection are applicable for cross referencing outside, societal conditions and for examination of the thinking and being of self. The prominence of its underlying occurrence across divergent cultures reflects its importance in understanding cultural similarities and our very humanity. Some of the oldest models on the matrix of four were used to understand the microcosm of ourselves through the ages.

The fact that polarity is often used to communicate and speculate without being realized is reflective of its consistency as an underlying thought process. People express contrast in singular polarity and in the duality of polarity, many times without even realizing it. The use of the matrix of four, the philosophy of the duality of polarity in everything from architecture, to observations of nature, to philosophical conjecture is longstanding and yet frequently unnoticed altogether underneath the specific discourse. Only when realized is the matrix of four, the philosophy of the duality of polarity truly useful despite being frequently utilized.

The duality of polarity has been essential to building structures over our heads and to understanding the operating function inside our heads since before the Egyptians erected the four sided base of their pyramids. The duality of polarity is physically represented in the architectural formation of such a square base. It is valuable as a basis physically in building the pyramids as it is in building on and understanding ideas. The four sides of the Egyptian pyramids actually have eight facets when more thoroughly examined from the sky, much like most four sided mandalas actually have eight subtleties when the in-betweens are noted.

The Egyptians erected some of the most outstanding architecture on the planet and they also expressed some of the most powerful ideas and inventions such as coming up with pen and paper and practicing meditation. The statues of the sitting Egyptians of reverence possibly depicts the meditation position. The many depictions of meditative movement similar to yoga positions backs up the idea the Egyptians were meditating.

The Egyptians also presented the idea of four basic personality types as did the Sumerians possibly before them. The idea of the four humors is likely extrapolated from the idea of the four elements, fire, air, water and earth. The four humors was used a basis for the ancient Egyptian medicinal perspective as well as cultural perspective through the character assessment of individuals. The Egyptians noted four basic personalities five thousand years ago partly in correspondence to physical attributes and wellbeing.

The mentality of an individual was considered reflective of one's physicality. The four humors begin in representation of the four vital fluids of the body, related to the four universal elements. They are blood, phlegm, yellow bile and black bile. Overall health and overall mental stability were thought to be related to the four vital fluids and four elements resulting in the four temperaments as later developed by the Ancient Greeks.

The ancient healers theorized that imbalance in the four humors resulted in different illnesses and behaviors, one's temperament. Hippocrates proposed that imbalance of the four humors influenced one's physical and mental wellness. He related these four qualities of being through the duality of polarity noting one could be balanced or out of balance via the matrix of hot and dry, hot and moist, cold and dry or cold and moist.

Hippocrates further adapted and expanded these ideas later in his presentation of cheerful, somber, enthusiastic and calm. And many more did the same after him, most significantly Galen, a second century physician and philosopher who influenced subsequent medicine for centuries. Galen noted the related set of four in sanguine, choleric, melancholic and phlegmatic.

The medical theory of elements and fluids in relation to organs might only be one layer of understanding, or a transitory understanding of the specifics of illness. The correlations between an individual's bodily fluids and their mentality or personality might not be reliable at all. Yet the fact that the summation of these implemented the matrix of four and the duality of polarity, concerning the basis of our physicality and mentality indicates its importance in relation to at least how we think. The idea itself while not necessarily totally reliable, reliably points to another significant instance of the matrix of four and the duality of polarity exploring our mentality and reflective of our mentality. The matrix of four and the duality of polarity were part of basic biological and psychological theory thousands of years ago exemplifying its ancient intrinsic importance in our thinking and being.

In ancient Egypt, with roots possibly in earlier traditions, the four basic personality types related to the four humors were reflected through the symbolism of animals. The lion was related to blood and boldness. The eagle was related to phlegm and far sight. The ox was related to black bile and sturdiness. The human was related to yellow bile and humaneness.

The ancient symbolism corresponds with the biblical verse of Ezekiel describing a vision of the same idea based on four. Ezekiel's vision of the Merkaba or the chariot of ascension is often suggested to be a secret description of a meditation on the four base chakras; the third eye, throat, heart and sacrum chakras. If such a secret meditation exists it likely originated in Egypt and perhaps elsewhere before that and would explain the controversy and occasional secrecy surrounding the Ezekiel text. Ezekiel sees the Merkaba or chariot of ascension, made of four wheels, driven by four beings, each with four wings and four faces; of a man, an ox, an eagle and a lion. The Merkaba symbol is discussed further in Chapter 6. Tummo meditation from Tibet focuses on spinning these four chakras like wheels of a chariot. Tummo meditation is the meditation of psychic heat.

"As for the likeness of their faces, they four had the face of a man and the face of a lion, on the right side: and they four had the face of an ox on the left side; they four also had the face of an eagle." ~Ezekiel 1:10

"This was the appearance and structure of the wheels: They sparkled like chrysolite, and all four looked alike. Each appeared to be made like a wheel intersecting a wheel."

~Ezekiel 1:16

The four evangelists of the Bible also share these symbols, Matthew's symbol is man, Mark the lion, Luke the ox and John the eagle. These four animals correlate Egyptian ideas with biblical verse as well as to similar astrological symbolism. The four fixed signs of astrology, as opposed to the mutable signs and cardinal signs, are Aquarius, Leo, Taurus and Scorpio.

The matrix of four and the duality of polarity have been used for millennia to point out personality types, personas and behaviors and to possibly hint at other concepts, perhaps those of biblical and astrological significance. And the frequency itself is perhaps indicative of patterns of shared thinking and being more than the related examples. Countless have pointed to an order of four in understanding people's mentality, based on the four temperaments and the duality of polarity. And despite its frequency of use the duality of polarity and matrix of four still often goes unsaid.

Plato described four personality types; artistic, sensible, intuitive and reasoning. Aristotle developed on the idea of four personality types as well; iconic, pistic, noetic and dianoetic. He also pointed to four sources of happiness; hedone (pleasure), propraieteri (acquiring assets), ethikos (moral virtue) and dialogike (logical investigation). Aristotle further speculated there were four causations; material cause, formal cause, moving cause and the final cause. These were said to be a way to understand changes and shifts in objects and subjects.

Four was and is intrinsic in understanding ourselves. Into the twentieth century German philosopher Eric Adickes explored four world views; doctrinaire, skeptical, traditional and innovative. These four perspectives are formed in the duality of polarity, the innovative being the distinct part to the set.

The philosopher and author P. D. Ouspensky wrote The Fourth Dimension. He also described four forms of development, the traditional three (fakir, monk, yogi) and the fourth way, the most distinct and developed, utilizing intuition. He described four mind states, the sleep state, wake state, self-awareness and objective consciousness. This set of four can be related to the archetype of the four levels of consciousness originally depicted in Aum.

Whatever the variation of abstracts, whatever the labels, the matrix of four and the duality of polarity form an invariable way to understand multiple objects and subjects and ultimately our very thinking and being. Ouspensky stated psychology is the oldest science and that there are two forms of it. The misguided form we mostly see, that is based on discovery of being. And the bettered, rarer form based on discovery of consciousness or discovery of becoming.

"A religion contradicting science and a science contradicting religion are equally false."

~P. D. Ouspensky

Carl Jung based his presentation of personality types on the duality of polarity. Like Ouspensky he deduced an objective consciousness shared by all people clearly exemplified by the frequency of the matrix of four and the duality of polarity in mandala designs conceptualized by individuals. His ideas have been used to elaborate on the subjects of personality and mentality since. Jung posited that people interpret the world through four different psychic functions of the ego; feeling, intuition, thought and sensation. He also proposed that people react to the world as introverts or extroverts. He figured further dichotomies expressing that thinking and feeling were rational and based on judging, while sensation and intuition were irrational and based on perceiving. These dichotomous deductions on mentality are based on the ancient formula of the four humors and the philosophy of the duality of polarity, our archetypal mode of thinking, a recognized mandala.

The Myers Briggs system of personality indication developed independently at first and then along with Carl Jung's proposals. It is also based on dichotomies, or the duality of polarity, to source its personality indications. This system ultimately polarizes the entirety of Jung's presentation. There is first the extrovert/introvert polarization, then sensing/intuition, thinking/feeling and judging/perceiving. Originally Katherine Briggs noted there were four personality types; meditative, spontaneous, social and executive. Her daughter later developed it into the indicator it is today. Others have followed and expanded on the Myers Briggs system of personality indication, most all continuing to use dichotomous elements or the philosophy of the duality polarity.

Whether or not the indicators are entirely reliable as a judge of personality is arguable. Whether or not any of the personality systems based on four are on their own wholly or partially accurate as indicators of personality is inconsequential to what they reveal about our collective personality throughout recorded time; we constantly utilize polarity and/or the duality of polarity, often without realization of it. Separately these forms of character assessment assist in deduction of personalities, together they point to the significance of the duality of polarity as intrinsic in human contemplations. The fact that the matrix of four and the duality of polarity have been and continue to be integral in the assessment of human personality and behavior for the last five thousand years is a revelation of human nature, our character and thinking in and of itself. Consciousness is awareness of awareness. All of these systems are aimed at increasing consciousness.

Through this Carl Jung noted our shared brotherhood across space and time and individual and mass consciousness. In his many essays and thoughts, especially later in life, he frequently contemplated polarity, dichotomy, contrasts, opposites and their relationships. He presumed the greatest polarity on earth was in the human mind as the conscious and unconscious of the individual and collective.

He also proposed that the male unconscious had a feminine psyche within it; the anima. And the female unconscious had a masculine psyche within it; the animus. Jung further conceived the shadow of self, the part of our consciousness which is unknown to us and can be destructive and occasionally productive. He proposed that people are capable of dealing with their shadows in one of four ways; denial, projection, integration and/or transmutation. This Jungian model is concerned with dealing with the unknown aspects of consciousness. He termed these unknowns as the Shadow. One can act in denial, projection, integration, or transmutation of the unknown shadow of self-consciousness and theoretically mass consciousness also. In the process of developing consciousness there is always a point in which the tumult and turmoil of the individual or collective climb is too much, where shadows are faced and many people turn back or stay still, but transcending it though transmutation results in a newness beyond the tumult.

Carl Jung coined the term quarternity meaning a four-sided figure or statement that symbolizes psychological totality or wholeness; such as that depicted in the four ways of expressing our unknown inner selves. A quarternity represents four parts toward understanding the whole, otherwise known as the matrix of four, the philosophy of the duality of polarity. His last major work, Mysterium Coniunctionis, an Inquiry into the Separation and Synthesis of Psychic Opposites in Alchemy, was focused on opposites and contrasts. Mysterium Coniunctionis means mysterious consciousness.

"The factors which come together in the coniunctio are conceived as opposites, either confronting one another in enimity or attracting one another in love. To begin with they form a dualism; for instance the opposites are humidum (moist)/siccum (dry), frigidum (cold)/ calidum (warm), superiora (upper, higher)/inferiora (lower), spiritus-anima (spirt-soul)/corpus (body), coelum (heaven)/terra (Earth), ignis (fire)/aqua (water), bright/dark, agens (active)/patiens (passive), volatile (volatile, gaseous)/fixum (solid), pretiosum (precious, costly; also carum, dear)/vile (cheap, common), bonum (good)/malum (evil), manifestum (open)/occultum (occult;also celatum, hidden), oriens (East)/occidens (West), vivum (living)/mortuum (dead, inert), masculus (masculine)/foemina (feminine), Sol/Luna." ~Carl Gustav Jung, Mysterium Coniunctionis

Sometimes polarity is absolute and sometimes it is relative. Polarity is so prevalent that even where it is not necessarily accurately applicable it is conceptualized as the swiftest and simplest way to communicate ideas. Just as alchemists used to speak of attempting to "square the circle" to understand the chaotic unity of totality by way of a set of four elements, the duality of polarity assists in beginning such understanding as well. Carl Jung identified four as containing and representing a quality shared by humanity, the matrix of four, the philosophy of the duality of polarity.

The mysterious and prized philosopher's stone of alchemists was said to have four parts. Some alchemy notes state there were rather four philosopher's stones; mineral, vegetable, magical and angelical. Alchemists sought the philosopher's stone as part of their secret quest to turn lead into gold and also, alternatively, to secretly transform dull thought into golden enlightenment.

Carl Jung tried to better people through a process he called individuation in which a person was taught to understand the reality of self and the world instead of simply being an unknowing subject unconsciously influenced and guided by the others in the world. Singular polarity is like asking, 'What is and what is not?' The duality of polarity asks 'What is and what isn't? What was and what can be?' Both Carl Jung and alchemy aspects were based on development of self, on becoming.

Meditations in tai chi and chi gung and yoga all point to man as a centrifuge or conductor of energy in the form of the duality of polarity at its basis. Such meditative movements and other meditations refer to being grounded to the flow of Earth energy and being attached to universal energy. Both energies have inward and outward flows and we slightly intermingle these energies each going in and out like electricity. Being grounded or rooted comes first and then being light or being integrated with light.

Singular polarity is often insufficient to explain natural phenomenon. It is often divisive and limiting when applied to social and political phenomenon, while the duality of polarity is capable of providing contrast and understanding of wholeness. One form of the duality of polarity or another is a constant from the Egyptian four humors, to Taoist meditation, to Jungian psychology in deciphering the commonality of our thinking and being, our consciousness, our awareness of self and surroundings.

People think in polarity to comprehend and communicate. The duality of polarity can be used in this way and also can be used to extrapolate and dissect. Often just one polarity is immediately recognizable while the pairing polarity might remain camouflaged. The frequency of the matrix of four, the philosophy of the duality of polarity is repeated in theology and philosophy from most every culture including the mysterious Alchemists who attempted to link the contrasting studies of science and spirituality to perform external and internal transformations.

The matrix of four, the philosophy of the duality of polarity represents psychological and mathematical completeness. In geometry a three dimensional object can be depicted using at minimum four points. It is mathematical certainty that four points is the minimum number required to portray a three dimensional object. In the same way that four points is the minimum number required to provide clarity to geometrical structure, four points is the minimum number required to provide clarity to psychological structure.

In geometry one point is a location, two points is a line, three points is the minimum number for an area of a field or plane and four points is the minimum number of points required to mathematically depict a three dimensional object. The matrix of four is symbolic for completion and assists in understanding objects and subjects as complicated and diverse as geometry and psychology.

The importance of the following set of four cannot be understated. This mathematical set of four is so primal that just like Aum or Yin Yang it could be argued the Matrix of Four is based on its structure. In geometry there are four ways to understand objects. The four ways to view any three dimensional object are as a point, line, plane or volume, each view potentially expanding perspective in its own way. Often, outside of mathematics, people will view the same situation and because one is contemplating the point and the other the plane if you will, they get caught up in distinctions of differing perspectives, instead of realizing their viewing the same thing, only in differing ways. Considering perspective in this way can assist in bringing people together.

"There are always four ways to look at any three-dimensional structure: as points, lines, areas, and volumes, or as corners, edges, faces, and from the center outward." Michael Schneider, Mathematician

One of the oldest numerological ideas that fused mathematical absolutes with spiritual understanding is the Tetraktys or tetrad. The ancient symbol, made up of a ten pointed triangular shape of four rows of 1, 2, 3 and 4 dots. One layer of it represents the mathematical absolute of four ways to perceive, via one dot signifying a point, two signifying a line, three the minimal number of points required for a plane, and four the minimum number of points required for three dimensional structure.

With roots in Egypt mystery schools the symbol was revered by Pythagoras and the Pythagoreans as representative of god and a key to understanding all things and is related to the four letter word for God, the Tetragrammaton and is often used in correlation with the Tree of Life of the Qabalah. In the Tetraktys is the counterintuitive reasoning that four equates to ten in the 4+3+2+1 row depiction, and another example of four being representative of completion. Through it was born the Pythagorean cosmology based on four parts; unity, dyad of limit/unlimit, harmony and kosmos.

The Tetraktys is said to represent creation, similarly to Tai Ji theory, via one point manifesting, two, two manifesting three, and then four and then the myriad things. Other Eastern Esoteric ideas that relate to the Tetraktys and its four rows of ten points at least on a subtle level to what are known as the ten divisions of the universe; the four cardinal points, four midway points, the zenith and the nadir.

"Bless us, divine number, thou who generated gods and men! O holy, holy Tetractys, thou that containest the root and source of the eternally flowing creation! For the divine number begins with the profound, pure unity until it comes to the holy four; then it begets the mother of all, the all-comprising, all-bounding, the first-born, the never-swerving, the never-tiring holy ten, the keyholder of all." ~Pythagorean Prayer

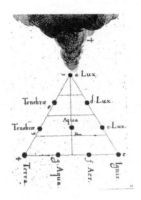

Chapter 5

The Exclusion of Four

"There are three. But where is the fourth?" ~Carl Jung, concerning many subjects

The exceptional aspects of the matrix of four, the philosophy of the duality of polarity is notable in physical and mathematical absolutes, in spirituality and theology, in the cross reference of information and in understanding our mentality. Perhaps the most magical aspects of the matrix of four are the mathematical ones. In the set of the first four numbers and all other numbers, four is distinct as the first non-prime. 1 is distinct as well as neither prime nor composite, for oneness just is. 2 and 3 are prime numbers, they have no divisors but 1 and themselves. 4 is the first composite as it has the additional divisor of 2. 4 is distinct as the first composite number.

There are five possible combinations to any set of four. All parts might be the same, AAAA. One might be unique and three might be the same, AAAB. There might be two like parts and two other like parts, AABB. There might be two matching parts and two other unlike parts, AABC. And all four parts might be different, ABCD. Many times one part of the set is distinct on one level or another, like 4 being the first composite number. Frequently there are different ways to decipher which type a set of four may be. Many times the fourth part of a set is distinct and developed, as well as being overlooked, obscured behind some veil and practically omitted altogether. Sometimes the duality of polarity is naturally, philosophically, and mathematically notable, and yet still ignored, as if not there, out of some traditional celebration of a singular polarity or a trinity. Or a fear of four.

There is no point in conjuring the duality of polarity or insisting upon the significance of the quantity of four. It distracts from the process of the philosophy of the duality of polarity; understanding. The human mind constantly consistently singularly polarizes the relativity of systems, without understanding the entirety of the situation or comprehending the duality of polarity. People polarize objects and subjects without thinking, while utilization of the duality of polarity requires thinking. Sometimes people think in polarity, or it is just how we think when we are passively and not actively thinking. Determining polarity is sometimes the best way to understand the extremes then the in-betweens can be noted. However when people polarize without realization they are doing so, without the duality of polarity, without seeking the in-betweens, understanding is restricted.

George Orwell coined the term doublethink in his work of political fiction, *1984*. Doublethink separates understanding and negatively polarizes without looking for the in-betweens. This results in believing two oppositions equate and believing one can only possibly think in one of two opposite directions. The duality of polarity expands thinking, but mere doublethink separates and limits.

When there are two major and two minor parts to a set of four, like the Ying Yang, the two minor parts are easily missed, instigating doublethink. When there are four similar parts to a set one or another might be missed or obscured. When there are four different parts to a set it is difficult to eliminate one or another and yet it happens. When there is one distinct part to a set of four, which is often the case, it is the easiest part to hide or omit.

There are many reasons for the tendency to obscure or eliminate a part of sets. Generally, the same individuals and institutions which would benefit from doublethink, or people thinking less, take part in elimination of parts to sets. Fictionally this idea is represented in *1984* as the institution in control sought to instill doublethink.

Sometimes people are simply afraid of four and the fourth part, out of tradition. In numerous Asian languages the word four is a homonym with the word death. People frequently equate the number with death and fear it and avoid it as death. In Asia tetraphobia, fear of four, is commonplace. People avoid the number so extensively it is omitted in elevators, in buildings and hospital room numbers across Asia. In Mandarin, Japanese, Vietnamese, and Korean the words death and four sound the same and the number is scorned as some in the west scorn thirteen, which coincidently is 1 and 3. The homonym is one reason why three or any other number is more desirable than four in some parts of the world.

Perhaps one of the most profound examples of the removal of a fourth part of a set is displayed in an old image and corresponding ancient adage from Asia. This image was heavily influenced by the tendency to consciously and unconsciously omit the number four and identify with the number three, going so far as to exclude the obvious and celebrated fourth part to the set. The homonym might be the main reason one of the most highly regarded images and adages across much of Asia is distorted, with the fourth part missing.

The adage and image of The Wise Monkeys is one of the most profound examples of the matrix of four. Typically it is displayed in a set of three. Hear No Evil, See No Evil and Speak No Evil are three monkeys in a row, one covering its eyes, the other covering its ears and the last covering its mouth. The three wise monkeys most commonly depicted in the adage are reflective of human characteristics, mostly unwise. The adage of the Wise Monkeys likely originates from ideas of Confucius. The Chinese philosophies ultimately migrated to Japan. And in Japanese the word not, and the word monkey are homonyms, possibly where the word play with the imagery originates.

"Look not at what is contrary to propriety; listen not to what is contrary to propriety; speak not what is contrary to propriety; make no movement which is contrary to propriety." ~Confucius, Analects of Confucius

The idea of the Wise Monkeys is likely derived from this four sided Confucius notion. The adage and image normally presents just the three monkeys, likely because of the aversion of four in the area of its origin and prominence, and potentially in relation to other philosophies which valued three, and the unsaid fourth. There are many lessons and reflections which can be gained from the adage and corresponding image aside from that alliterated by Confucius, both for individual and collective consciousness. Because the three monkeys limit themselves in one way or another, none seem wise at all. Ignoring inconsequence is wise however ignoring evil is a dangerous ignorance. The Three Wise Monkeys look dumb, deaf and blind, especially with knowledge of the hidden fourth monkey.

The seldom displayed missing part, the fourth monkey, is known as Fear No Evil or Do No Evil and is the only one which seems wise at all. The fourth monkey holds its abdomen, symbolic for center and the point where all movement originates in Asian cultures. The fourth monkey looks, listens, speaks, but fears no evil and perhaps thusly, does no evil. The other three are afraid of what they might see, hear, or say. Fear no evil is the distinct 1 next to the 3, as well as the distinct composite of the set. There are many ways to interpret the multiple layers of the image and adage symbolism. The immediate interpretation being that the Wise Monkeys represent the idea to avoid watching, listening, speaking or doing evil and a more elaborate interpretation being they represent the duality of polarity of consciousness, along with the distinct and developed fourth part.

"The most dangerous person is the one who looks, listens, thinks and observes." ~Bruce Lee

The missing fourth monkey reveals hidden truth, the power of hidden truth, the reason for hiding truth and exemplifies how to counter untruth. The absence of the fourth wise monkey helps to point out the very lesson the wise monkeys maxim imparts: Observe reality and openly communicate with others about the nature of the conditions around you. By observing and speaking without fear, you will find what is hidden, often by way of what is already known.

In much of Asia four is a homonym with death which also inspired the elimination of its mention, like thirteen. A similar numerological implication of death is noted in Western cultures. In The Bible, four is the number of apocalyptic horsemen who bring death to the world. Four is symbolic of completion, death being the ultimate completion. Some systems denote three parts to life; birth, life and death. And some people say that death comes in threes, pointing to a frequent aversion and power to the number as well.

When evil is about, the only way to cancel it is to look, listen, speak up about it and cease support of it without fear. Stand up forthrightly, unafraid. Do not cooperate with evil, but face it head on. When evil becomes institutionalized, by governments and corporations, it must be confronted by the people with foreknowledge of their surroundings and conditions. Only by using the senses and refusing to serve evil, can one make monkey-work out of canceling the evil that lurks behind the shadows of our society.

The political and social lessons of The Wise Monkeys reveal a pattern at play and reveals how to raise the bar to the pattern. If we remain in the hyper politicized and institutionalized construct we will inevitably be reacting out the simple layer of The Wise Monkeys, playing the game if you will, at best being a peaceful warrior and righteous rebel that is The Fourth Monkey and as the number suggest, most likely being most frequently one or the other Monkeys, the deaf, dumb, blind, the idiot, zealot and elitist.

The pattern is revealed in the monkey mind relations of the external and exoteric worlds. The format to develop ourselves internally and esoterically is also revealed via the duality of polarity, viewing the concept of collective relations with perspective geared toward internal refinement. The best way to develop ourselves and then raise the bar of our relationships and our surroundings is to develop self.

How do we practice self-development? If we release the potential of The Wise Monkeys the process is revealed. The first step is to focus, to open your eyes and maintain a steady focus on practice. The second step is take responsibility for all around you and not be deaf to the lessons offered and potentials revealed. The third step is to care to elevate others, and care to share information on the process with those around you. With steady focus of vision, clarity of hearing, and caring to share comes love for of The Fourth Monkey.

At the heart of the heroic nature of The Fourth Monkey is the contrast of seeking to do no wrong. If we imagine only doing things we know are not wrong we can relate to the loving nature of The Fourth Monkey. Many institutionalized warriors will do what they believe is right, not The Fourth Monkey. The fourth monkey only acts on what is not wrong.

The somewhat hidden esoteric self-development layering within The Wise Monkeys symbolism is mirrored in The Four Powers of The Sphinx in Eliphas Levi's work Key to The Mysteries. The Four Powers of The Sphinx are Knowledge, Will, Courage, and Silence, corresponding to the four classical elements, air, fire, water, and earth. These powers or attributes are the contrasts of the Three Wise Monkeys failing and an enhancements of The Fourth Monkey, the righteous rebel.

There are many celebrated sets of three and for various reasons, the unspoken fourth. Essentially four holds the spiritual and silent aspect and with that, death, but more specifically the beyond. Many Hindus celebrate trinities of sorts and yet acknowledge a fourth part, reasoning it should be unspoken, as the supreme ultimate truth, the transcendence and silence of oneness behind the veil. This comes from the belief that the supreme ultimate truth cannot be spoken and once it is spoken it is not the absolute supreme ultimate truth.

In Tibetan medicine there are three methods of diagnosis and of course the potential unsaid fourth aspect of intuitive and spiritual recognition. The three methods are observation of the patient and the patient's urine, listening to the pulse, and communication of questions concerning the patient's lifestyle. Extrapolating from these methods of diagnosis, there are also four related methods for healing; the vibration of sound, the vibration of light, ingestion of medicine, and spiritual healing which could be anything from massage to prayer.

During the European Inquisitions, people were imprisoned, tortured and killed for questioning the dominant religious presentation of one God made up of the holy trinity. To suggest there was anything other than three parts to one God resulted in a heretical death sentence. Nontrinitarians did not follow the institutional doctrine celebrating the trinity of the Father, Son and the Holy Ghost. Mother or mother Earth is an obvious omission from this set. Most nontrinitarians simply believed in the oneness of one god.

Michael Servetus was a theologian and physician who lived in the time when alternate thinking pertaining to the holy three was punishable. First his effigy was burned and then Michael himself was burned at the stake in 1553, for writing books on Unitarian philosophy that stated Trinitarian beliefs were not biblical in origin, but were deceptions of certain Greek philosophies. For whatever reason, perhaps simply as a form of control, Trinitarian perspective dominated and was violently enforced.

Neither with those nor with the others, in all I agree and dissent; in all part of truth and part of error must be seen." ~Michael Servetus

Perhaps the insistence of three was based on the frequently celebrated trinity of self; mental, physical and spiritual. However this trinity is a duality of polarity with an omission, a misnomer as much as the story of the three wise men. Nowhere does it say the number of wise men to visit baby Jesus was three and nowhere is the relationship of mental, physical and spiritual complete. In fact the Hindu idea of Purusha and Prakrti breaks down this example of the duality of polarity and is an idea similar to the Yin Yang. There is matter, nature and contrastingly there is spirit, consciousness. Hindu tradition states that understanding and distinguishing this set of four Purusha and Prakti relieves suffering and leads to knowledge. The knowledge of this set of four provides alleviation of suffering though consideration of the totality of a thing or situation. This set of four also provides a step by step progression to instigate and develop consciousness. The first step is to enliven the mental aspect, the second step is to develop the physical, and thirdly one develops the spiritual so that one can connect with and will oneself onto the natural. No connection with nature and no influence on anything can occur without development and understanding of the four aspects.

Mental conditioning and development can be accomplished through expanding and focusing one's attention and considering objects and subjects utilizing the four forms of information. Purification and strengthening of the physical is most efficiently done through high quality vegan diet and exertion. Meditation as well as assisting others in need, develops the spiritual aspect. Chi gung and the Five Tibetan Rites of Rejuvenation (and occasionally the sixth) have proven to be especially powerful in developing intuitive consciousness and the integration of mental, physical and spiritual aspects. Only when one develops oneself can one integrate oneself with the natural aspect and will oneself upon it.

The natural has been omitted from consideration in this set of four, predominantly seen as a trinity. The fourth part among the set of physical, mental and spiritual is predominantly excluded and as evident by the way most of nature is treated, is unconsidered in most endeavors. The omission of this fourth part, lacking consideration of the natural aspect, has led to immense suffering, through inconsiderate destruction of nature. The trinity of mental/physical/spiritual, or mind/body/spirit is incomplete without the natural, nature, Mother Earth. When the natural is included in the set, traditionally viewed as containing only three, the duality of polarity is evident and obvious.

Many sets of self are presented as being made up of only three parts. Some refer to the mental, physical, and spiritual aspects. Others refer to the three parts as mental, emotional and physical. In our world today the fourth part, be it natural or emotional or spiritual is frequently omitted from consideration. Incidentally the heart and mind connection of emotion and thought has been proven repeatedly, biologically indicative in the presence of heart neurons. Thinking and feeling are of the same aspect, the mental. Our reckoning ability has logical and emotional layers like the physical layer contains skeletal and arterial layers. Logical thought is more stable, emotional thoughts are wavy like water, subject to tidal and elemental influences. Each are codependent.

Perhaps during no other time in history is consideration of and attention to the fourth part to this set more important. The natural world, of which our physical, mental and spiritual are part of and dependent on, without which there would be no development, is being destroyed and is frequently left unconsidered in its entirety. Arguably this fourth part, the natural aspect, has been unconsidered and omitted from this familiar set of four in order to maintain the status quo, in this case, potentially to maintain the status quo for the energy oligarchs as is the debate over the rise in temperature equating to human induced environmental destruction.

Society largely omits consideration of both the spiritual and the natural aspects preferring instead to concentrate on the simply the physical/material. And when the mental aspect is considered it is so only in limited layers, emotion and intuition are mostly not considered as valid. Spiritual and natural subjects and objects are in the same way presented as being irrelevant and further unconsidered by most. The physical and mental aspects of self are easily noted while the spiritual and natural aspects are easily hidden. This has resulted in the suggestion that spirit is nonexistent and nature does not require consideration. Whereas in reality spirit is within us and nature is us. And in the same way we tend to separate ourselves

68

from nature when not acting as its custodian, when we don't act as a caretaker for our own spirituality we become equally disconnected.

The name Jesus Christ is a combination of Hebrew and Greek words, contrasting cultures of the time in which he lived. YHWH or Joshua is the original Hebrew name and Christos is Greek word for anointed. The life of Jesus, on one layer, symbolizes the four or depending on how on looks at it, five stages of initiation one must go through toward individuation. First is nativity or rebirth, the beginning a meditation practice for example. Second is baptism or purification, expelling negativity physically and energetically. Thirdly is transmutation, the transformation and application of the practice into positivity for self and others, symbolized in the healings and teachings. The fourth stage is the final payment and final purification of karma, symbolized in the crucifixion. And after the final payment is rebirth in mastery.

Older Greek ideas and ideas of other origins were absorbed into the new ideas of Christianity. Historically speaking, new religions frequently adopted ideas of older religions/cultures and/or the new religion warred with the old theology. The Greeks exchanged philosophy with many cultures and the entirety of what is called Greek Philosophy is one elaborate affair covering a wide spectrum of subject matter, some obviously, influenced by Egyptian traditions, including the concept of the four humors.

One of the most influential understandings from Greek philosophy is a dialogue based on the matrix of four and the philosophy of the duality of polarity. It contains the matrix, including the distinction of the fourth part, the impulse to be rid of the fourth part and a measure of individual and the collective consciousness.

This Socratic dialogue is an allegory so insidiously extrapolative of the human condition that it remains influential to this day, especially in Orwell's *1984* and obviously in the film The Matrix. The dialogue is called The Allegory of the Cave. The allegory begins in a dark cave, reflective of individual and political consciousness and predicaments. And it ends in explaining the inclination to eliminate the distinct fourth character, the hero and righteous rebel.

Socrates was one of the most influential and eccentric Greek philosophers. His ideas have remained relevant for millennia yet he never penned a word. People wrote of him and his ideas. Stories of him speak of him teaching openly on the streets to all individuals. Plato wrote the most about him as well as authoring his own ideas.

The philosophy behind the Allegory of the Cave has been endlessly integrated into everything from politics to entertainment and perhaps even religion. The duality of polarity is a subtle and yet intrinsic part of dialogue within the Allegory, but the discussion of the elimination of the distinct fourth part is stark. The correlations and comparisons in reality to the allegory are endless as if there were a thousand caves to leave. But it is certainly reflective of any institution or group seeking to control, including the very real story of Michael Servetus who questioned the holy trinity. And just as the potential energy oligarchies would like to omit consideration of the natural and just as people who wanted to kill Michael Servetus for suggesting there was possibly more to the story, the three character types in The Allegory of the Cave end up wanting to eliminate the fourth, distinct character, so as to maintain the status quo.

The Allegory of the Cave in Plato's The Republic was originally written around 380 BC. In The Republic Plato describes four types of government; monarchy, oligarchy, tyranny, and democracy. The Allegory of the Cave is a discussion on human mentality and the body politic, our thinking and being. There are four types of people in the cave, four, based on the duality of polarity, though nowhere in the text are the characters overtly counted. In the cave there are the captors and captives. The captives in the cave are controlled and know nothing in life but the cave, worse they only know one wall of the cave. The captors use a fire to cast shadows on the wall the prisoners face to keep them captivated and distracted by a made up reality. Among the captives there are the chained and the unchained. The chained are held in place so that they can only look straight ahead and are convinced of the reality and moreover importance of the shadows. The unchained are transfixed with the images and convinced of the reality and moreover importance of the shadows to the point they don't need chains. They are held by shadows, like elephants on to a string. Both the chained and unchained captives have no interest in their actual existence as captives in a cave. They are not conscious, they are not aware of self or their surroundings, or the captors, they are only aware of and concerned with the shadows.

The captors hold the captives with shadows, as distractions. There are the chained captives, the unchained captives and the captors who hold them. The fourth character in the allegory, the fourth distinct part of the set, is the freed prisoner. The freed prisoner, after being in the cave his whole life, finds himself aboveground and is at first pained by sunlight and then begins to see. First he sees only shadows as that is what he is accustomed, then reflections, then the objects casting shadows and then finally the total of his surroundings, himself, others and the stars and the sun. The freed prisoner learns about sunlight and the dependence of all things on it. He learns about the basic tenets of reality and that the sun is the true light, not the captors' fire. The freed prisoner learns about simple conditions of reality and the things which the captors' shadows represented. He becomes conscious and understands his place in the world. He realizes he was deceived his whole life and that everyone he had ever known from the cave is imprisoned and deceived as well. And he has to return.

After deliberation the freed prisoner returns and attempts to inform the captives of their predicament and by that free them. The chained and unchained captives scorn the freed prisoner for not being able to see in the dark cave, his eyes having adjusted to daylight.

Eventually they want to eliminate the freed prisoner for revealing their predicament to them, for upsetting the status quo, even though they are held captive by it. The controlling captors of course seek to eliminate him or anyone who questions and exposes the cave system for what it is. There are many layers to the Allegory of the Cave which are relevant to a myriad of other philosophies and stories. But the depiction of four characters and four types of mentality is distinct, formed in terms of the matrix of four and the philosophy of the duality of polarity. The three characters being compelled to remove the fourth distinct type, the freed prisoner, the one who seeks to free the captives and show them true light as opposed to control them in the cave is reflective of how controlling institutions operate.

In the Allegory of the Cave the duality of polarity is apparent in the chained, the unchained, those acting to imprison and the one acting to set free. Throughout recorded time institutions have adopted and utilized ideas similar to or even from the Allegory of the Cave where portions of reality are omitted and portions of fiction are added. As a result the fourth part is practically always removed, the duality of polarity hidden for the captors' ends. One and sometimes two parts to the set are frequently eliminated instigating doublethink or an allegorical celebration of shadows. In the same way as the likes of Donald Rumsfeld would rather people not think about unknown knowns, the secrets some know and others don't, society today too, most all people in most states, figurative captives and captors would rather not consider the spiritual aspects or natural aspects either.

The Allegory of the Cave is reflective of the internal mind state as well as the external state of government or society. It is reflective of deceptive control on micro and macro levels. Internally there are fears and blockages to being open minded and centered. In external reality such captors seek to control the opposition to their adopted position or thesis to eliminate the control the opposition. Control is covertly gained over opposition by presenting a limited thesis which will result in a predictable antithesis, other times they overtly, outright eliminate the opposition. For institutions, tetraphobia is commonplace. Institutions in control despise the idea of the fourth part, willing, the enlightened freed prisoner, the unafraid wise monkey, Fear No Evil. The fourth part in the subject of political thinking and being is the righteous rebel. Institutions cannot use the righteous rebel. Hence the elimination, as allegorically presented in the Allegory of the Cave and literally displayed in the traditional omission of the fourth part of the Confucius inspired adage of The Wise Monkeys. The tendency to eliminate or retain the secrecy of the fourth part, as well as reasoning to do so is presented within the framework of the allegory. The fourth part, the righteous rebel, Fear No Evil, is enlightened and unafraid and therefore powerful. The righteous rebel inspires development of individual and mass consciousness, internally and externally. The development of inward and outward consciousness always faces resistance within self and in society as well.

71

Institutions frequently operate in triangular or pyramidal fashion, in systems frequently based on three parts. Three points is enough for institutions and symbolizes a triangle and perhaps the three classes of institutions; religious, state, corporate. It is arguable that frequent elimination of the fourth part is done to restrict thinking and debate. For philosophically speaking the fourth part to many sets of the duality of polarity is distinct as the developed alternative. This is represented in the three branches of government of the United States of America; Representative, Judicial and Executive. The media is known as the fourth branch and at one time were, in general, a more skeptical and questioning check among the powers. The righteous rebels are like reporters and unafraid activists. Jesus and Gandhi were both righteous rebels of the highest order. And Nietzsche is famous for writing about being a righteous rebel in order to become an uberman.

It is simply a matter of fact that institutions promote the notion of three. Tetraphobia among institutions and the tendency to eliminate the fourth part is commonplace mainly because of the power of righteous rebel. The fourth part of the duality of polarity of thinking and being, the allegorical freed prisoner, is a threat to the lower forms of control. This institutional abhorrence for the fourth part is subtly depicted in *1984*. Elements of the Allegory of the Cave are so many in *1984* that it can be considered a direct descendant.

1984 takes place in a world where three super states are at war, where the sides shift as do accompanying lies. The people in the fictional oligarchy are forced to watch contrived images and news on telescreens which conversely watch and listen over them. The telescreens display shadows and most people are like the chained and unchained in the Allegory of the Cave, transfixed by shadows. Information is controlled and contrived by the captors of the story and forced upon everyone as reality. The main character realizes the lies. One of the original titles considered for *1984* was The Last Man in Europe. *1984* is a story of a freed prisoner.

"The solid world exists, its laws do not change. Stones are hard, water is wet, objects unsupported fall toward the Earth's center. With the feeling he was speaking to O'Brien and also that he was setting forth an important axiom, he wrote: Freedom is the freedom to say two plus two equals four. If that is granted all else follows." ~George Orwell, *1984*

The institutional insistence of three parts to sets is demonstrated in the story, while four types are described by the author. There are four types of people in *1984*; the Inner Party, the Outer Party, the Proles and the elusive Brotherhood. The main character is presented a revolutionary book, which had in fact been adopted by the established institution as controlled opposition. The first sentence of this book within the book describes three types of people in the world; the

72

High, the Middle and the Low similar to the Inner Party, Outer Party and Proles. The Brotherhood, which allegedly challenges the ruling institutions and the status quo is said to be made up of people who recognize the lies and corruption, correlates with the freed prisoners. The institution in control would rather eliminate the notion of the Brotherhood or control the Brotherhood as its opposition. There are other occurrences of four in the story and whether Orwell put them in purposefully or without realization is irrelevant to the fact that they are there. The story begins on April, 4, 1984 for instance.

In The Matrix, Neo is the freed prisoner, formerly wired into a technological cavern of fake being, a life of shadows, just like in the Allegory of the Cave. He is brought into the real world as the freed prisoner, who ultimately gains consciousness and returns to free the other prisoners. The technological control grid in the film is equivalent to the shadows on the wall displayed by the machines, representing the captors.

The political and actual representations are easy enough to quantify and the power of the freed prisoner or righteous rebel is recognizable throughout the world. One of the most important layers to the Allegory of the Cave and one of the most difficult layers to face is that of the personal layer of the cave within or the caves we make around us. The shadows are false evidence appearing real, fear. The outside world of fires and shadows often uses fear to steer, but inside fear is used the same. We all replay shadows to ourselves to keep the status quo inside so we don't have to face the reality of inside and outside. We all have our own personal caves where false evidence appearing real controls us. The freed prisoner, the righteous rebel, is powerful in the real world and within our own real worlds, in leading us out of our own personal caves, toward enlightenment.

Many Socratic dialogues and Greek philosophies are related to the matrix of four and the duality of polarity similarly to the Allegory of the Cave and its many decedents. The Analogy of the Divided Line is directly related to the matrix of four, the philosophy of the duality of polarity.

Socrates divided information into four parts, based on the matrix of four, the philosophy of the duality of polarity, thousands of years before Donald Rumsfeld proposed his eloquent and yet watered down version lacking the ultra-important fourth part to the set. Socrates noted here is the tangible, a tree for instance (DE) and there are reflections of the tangible (CD), like the tree's reflection in a pond. There is also the intangible, like numbers (BC) and finally reflections of the intangible (AB), algebraic equations for instance. The largest part of the set is the tangible and the smallest, most elusive part is the reflections of the intangible.

The Analogy of the Divided Line correlates with The Allegory of the Cave, and Socrates' further deduction, that there were four types of thought processes; picture thinking, belief, reason and wisdom, wisdom being the distinct and developed fourth part. All are further examples of the matrix of four and the duality of polarity utilized in understanding human thinking and being. Plato's Theory of Forms, which explores the distinction between reality and ideas, or objects and subjects, is related to the Allegory of the Cave. The Metaphor of the Sun is related as well, which deduces the Sun to be the source of knowledge.

The Socratic dialogue of Meno's Slave and the Square is abstractly related to the duality of polarity and the elusive fourth part; the unknown knowns in the form of intuition. Mathematical reasoning is explored as well as learning and knowing. Meno's slave is said to be ignorant of math and Socrates is able to get him to recognize how to double the size of a square by drawing four squares and then drawing another square containing exactly double the area of the first square. Socrates debated with Meno that people don't learn things, but rather remember them, like intuition. Intuition is one form of unknown knowns and another possible reason for the elimination of the fourth part, as intuition leads to questioning everything, especially controlling powers. Perhaps as information was kept from Meno's slave for various reasons, the fourth part of the duality of polarity is obscured the same, for various reasons related to control and eliminate intuition and alternative.

Institutions of slavery thousands of years ago hid information from their slaves so that they would not seek to free themselves, for information will instigate such course of action. Meno likely kept many things hidden from his slaves, not just mathematics. Today the same restriction or narrowing of perspective takes place on as small a scale of an individual enslaving another to as grand an operation as controlling global relations and interactions.

There are several ways to look at state systems. A beginning contrast is the micro and macro or local and global context. Political science studies the complexities of state politics and international relations through levels of analysis. Graham T. Allison is a political scientist who wrote the highly influential Essence of Decision. In it he explored different causes for state decisions, especially in crisis, specifically the Cuban Missile Crisis. Originally he pointed out three levels of analysis, and later four levels were proposed. It is a way to observe the complex influences and reasoning behind international actions and relations by examining how and why, the causes and effects. It explores what is influential, and what influences are noticed as well as mostly unnoticed.

The relationships of states on the international stage are examined. Relationships and reasoning of organizations at home are examined. And the relationships between individuals at home are examined. The level of analysis originally left out of the examination is relationships of institutions or organizations on the international stage. In the levels of analysis the four points are influences of outside states, within state individual influences, within state institutional influences and outside state institutional influences.

"The essence of ultimate decision remains impenetrable to the observer – often even to the decider himself." ~John F. Kennedy

Narrowing perspective through compartmentalization and elimination of points has been taking place for millennia. Polarity is ubiquitous and it can be used to understand totality with the duality of polarity and also to be totally divisive as with doublethink. Examination of systems through the duality of polarity broadens thinking. Application of it whenever only two or three points are noted tends to lead to wider understanding. Incidentally Plato means broad. And whenever polarity limits options to either/or and whenever just three triangular notions are presented application of the duality of polarity can broaden understanding.

It is imperative to ask questions. It is imperative to ask pertinent and relative questions to discover hidden or omitted portions to ideas, sets and systems. The duality of polarity is ubiquitous however many things work on levels or by way of degrees and are contrasted or polarized only by way of our thinking. Many ideas, sets and systems are logical, philosophical and theological in their own right without so much of a suggestion of four or the duality of polarity. Some things are indeed made up of other numbers besides four or multiples of four and do not hold aspects of the duality of polarity at all. The duality of polarity is not the singular way to understand everything and it is not always the best way to understand anything. It is a good way to understand a great amount and it is possibly the best way to begin questioning and understanding most anything.

Scholars and philosophers have contemplated the universe in terms of the duality of polarity for millennia, many times without knowing or explaining knowing so. The matrix of four, the philosophy of the duality of polarity is at the basis of nearly everything from arithmetic to breath and detectable in the thinking of everyone from the poetic to the prophetic. The philosophy is based on absolutes, but not an absolute itself and still the duality of polarity can be efficiently applied to understand the thinking and being of people, a subject with very few, if any absolutes at all.

…ence seemed to be based on duality, on contrast. Either one was a man or one was a …, either a wanderer or sedentary burgher, either a thinking person or a feeling person - …e could breathe in at the same time as he breathed out, be a man as well as a woman, …erience freedom as well as order, combine instinct and mind. One always had to pay for one …th the loss of the other, and one thing was always just as important and desirable as the other." ~Herman Hesse, Narcissus and Goldmund

Chapter 6

Questions and Answers

"Is the universe eternal? Or not? Or both? Or neither? Is the universe finite? Or not? Or both? Or neither? Is the self identical with the body? Or is the self different from the body? Does the Tathagata (name Buddha used for himself meaning the one who has thus come and the one who has thus gone) exist after death? Or not? Or both? Or neither?" ~The Fourteen Unanswered Questions of Buddha.

The human body exhibits the duality of polarity through our four limbs, our right and left arms and right and left legs. Neural research concludes the main portion of the human brain is made up of right and left hemispheres, each side being slightly chemically different. The right side controls linear thinking, while the left side controls holistic thinking. There are however four main parts to the brain anatomically and systematically speaking. The human brain is made up of the two hemispheres of the Cerebrum, the Cerebellum, the Brain Stem, and the Diencephalon. It's theorized the human brain evolved by way of four main stages, each still a part of us. There is the reptilian brain based on survival, the old mammalian brain based on desires and impulses, the new mammalian brain based on just two things; prediction and comprehension. And the fourth most developed part is the prefrontal cortex in charge of elevated being and conscious compassionate commitment. Harnessing and controlling the three basic parts of the brain leads to more conscious self-control. The human heart similarly has four chambers. Abstractly we are consciousness vehicles operating in the formation of the duality of polarity. We have sympathetic and parasympathetic operating systems, for example we see automatically without thinking about it, but we must actively look. And we have a dominant and less dominant side. Much of our very biological makeup is based on the matrix of four and the duality of polarity.

Our eyes, through which we detect light, operate via the duality of polarity. When light enters the eyes images cross from one side to the other from upside down to right side up and back and forth. The light initially closes receptors so as to form an image instead of opening them, like a negative. Light and electricity are often compared and indeed work much the same way, in the duality of polarity. One of the most powerful meditations for grounding oneself functions on the duality of polarity and meditative energy works like light and electricity. Imagine grounding with the feminine earth, out flow from the root chakra, in flow from the soles of your feet. Then imagine universal masculine energy coming in through your crown, down your back and then up through your front back out the crown. Some meditation techniques consider that the energy coming above and below twists in a positive and negative dynamic just like the depiction of a double helix. These energies intersect and just slightly and intermix at the root chakra. The flows of the grounding meditation is a lot like positive and negative electrical flows and is a bit like light coming into our eyes.

The theories of special relativity and general relativity, as theorized by Albert Einstein, in part state that reality is four dimensional, made up of time, length, width and depth. Also he states there are four forms of fundamental force in the universe; weak nuclear force, strong nuclear force, electromagnetism and gravity. A fifth force is thought to exist and yet is undiscovered. Four is representative of completion in numerous systems from our physical composition, to the laws of the four dimensional universe and its four forces. Without the balance of these four forces life as we know it would not be possible. The matrix of four is physically and naturally exemplified in our inner microcosm and the celestial macrocosm and is spiritually and mentally recognized by many cultures throughout recorded time.

Our minds are wired to question, only frequently we ask limited questions. Curiosity is a quality shared by all, only many are trained not to be curious. We are capable of questioning everything in the four dimensions. Some questions are of physics and nature while others are about spiritual or mental applications. There are a few questions which all people have all posed since time immemorial. Some of the same questions have been asked, like those posed to and unanswered by Buddha, for millennia. They reveal our nature to question everything, even and perhaps especially the unanswerable. Sometimes answers are found. Einstein found many answers to his questions about the universe. Normally when questions are answered though, new questions arise. Some questions however are not worth asking and not worth pursuing like the fourteen unanswered questions of Buddha, also known as the imponderables. The Fourteen questions are actually four questions, three with four aspects and one with two. Despite Buddha's refusal to answer the questions they were still posed in the most developed manner possible, in four ways to form completion, in hopes of getting an answer.

Buddha believed people existed in either two states; in existence or nonexistence. Many people visited him with questions and these were said to be the only questions he did not answer. It is believed he thought the imponderables could never truly be answered and that they led to states of negativity and nonexistence, ultimately inconsequential to our earthly redicament of eliminating suffering and attaining enlightenment. Many questions are worth deliberation and elaboration because they are pertinent to our earthly predicament. But at least these four questions, the imponderables, were inconsequential to Buddha.

Questions are posed completely in four ways, as illustrated in the formation of the imponderables. The formation of the questions are valuable on their own and indicative of the matrix of four and the philosophy of the duality of polarity. Buddha is asked these four questions in the formation of the duality of polarity, with four important parts. Is it so? Is it not so? Is it both? Is it neither?

The very inquiry into the origins of human thinking and being is posed through the duality of polarity and yet it's most often considered via a singular polarity. Why are we the way we are? Are we the result of nature or nurture? The debate of nature versus nurture is mostly posed in a single distinct polarization. Yet the best answer supersedes the singular polarity and is traditionally philosophically viewed as a trinity of options, a synthesis of one and the other, of thesis and antithesis. And yet this is actually the matrix of four and the duality of polarity with the fourth part missing. It should be asked in the same philosophical formation as the imponderables, which despite Buddha's refusal to answer, were still posed in the most developed manner possible, in hopes of an answer.

Is human thinking and being the result of nature? Or nurture? Or both? Or neither? This idea may be explored in multiple ways and has roots among many disciplines. Questioning our thinking and being aim at providing evidence for an actual answer, however the pinnacle purpose of such debate is to understand the possibilities, the in-betweens, through the duality of polarity. Whenever the either/or option is put forth it is limited for there are always four possible present answers; one, the other, both and neither. In the case of nature versus nurture, the most sensible answer is both nature and nurture makes us who we are, but perhaps it is neither, perhaps other systems rather than biological or experiential are at play, like astrological systems for instance.

Does art reflect life or does life reflect art? This similarly philosophical question is aimed at its own answers, but yet is primarily based on understanding possibilities via the duality of polarity. There are four basic forms of answers to this question and those like it, and yet in typical form, only two or three are normally explored. The three comprised of one, the other or the combination of both, philosophically known as thesis, antithesis, and synthesis. There are the obvious two answers posed, one contrasting the other and a mixture is the third choice. The distinct fourth option, seemingly always left out, possibly because of its ability to shake the status quo is the unlimited alternative, the nullisis. In the philosophical set of thesis, antithesis and synthesis the distinct possibility is missing, the unlimited alternative, the neither option. The nullisis answer is outside the box, or outside the cave, thinking.

Nullisis can be abstractly compared to and understood through the four human blood types. In every dialectical discussion there is thesis, antithesis, synthesis and nullisis or A, B, AB, and O. Nullisis, neither, the unlimited alternative is complicated for it opens up every dialectic to any alternative. This philosophical distinction of the matrix of four, the philosophy of the duality of polarity, the unlimited alternative of nullisis is possibly the main reason for the ever elimination of the fourth part and celebration of three, the main reason for tetraphobia. Consideration of alternatives is similarly limited to one, the other and the combination, because the next option, neither, opens up the door to anything else. And entities seeking to control, during any time period, anywhere, would automatically prefer to eliminate the fourth part for it represents the unlimited alternative, while the either/or situation usually results in controllable back and forth combinations.

The origin of the celebrated triad of thesis, antithesis, synthesis, is often attributed to Georg Wilhelm Hegel, however he criticized what is now often called Hegelian Dialectic. Johann Gottlieb Fichte actually formed the original presentation. Hegel is known to have called the triad of thesis, antithesis and synthesis 'boring' and a 'lifeless schema.' Without nullisis, neither, the unlimited alternative, the commonly referenced philosophical triad is a lifeless schema for if one combines a wrong answer with the right answer a half correct solution might result.

Hegel did use and note a similar extrapolation of three; immediate, mediated and concrete. Critics note this trinity to be limited by way of assumptions and errors, soup in what is assumed to be concrete. Without nullisis or new information, one could possibly begin with information which is then countered by disinformation and ends up misinformation. Nullisis is needed. Nullisis is the distinct and developed fourth part, the essence of new thinking and being.

If mathematics can be considered beautiful, nullisis is beautifully illustrated through the most mysterious and elusive of all arithmetic equations, an imponderable of sorts itself. It is represented in one of the most mysterious equations of the most complicated of all numbers; zero. In fact there is no zero. Zero can never be physically represented and in the entire universe there is not one. Even in nothingness there is something. And through its cancellation is its verification. There are in fact zero zeros. Zero represents nothing and uncertainty, uncertainty similar to that of the unlimited alternative.

Mathematics seeks clear answers and in practically all arithmetic there are clear answers, but there is only one arithmetic equation that represents uncertainty and unlimited possibility, the nullisis. $0 + 0 = 0$, $0 - 0 = 0$, $0 \times 0 = 0$, but the answer to 0 divided by 0 is unlimited possibility reflective of nullisis. The answer to zero divided by zero is an undefined unknown. It is the only simple arithmetic equation to which the answer is unknown. A valid answer to this equation could be anything from zero to infinity, just the same as with nullisis, the unlimited alternative.

It is notable that in arithmetic division is the distinct operation. It represents sharing for one, and not necessarily what has come to be known as divisiveness.

The most sensible answers to both the debate of nature versus nurture and the question of art reflecting life or life reflecting art is synthesis, both. It is a combination of nature and nurture that makes us who we are. It is a balance of influences in art and life which influence one another. Art contains a spark of life, while life is artful. Nature and nurture, art and life, are inseparable like a swirling Yin Yang, contrasting syntheses. Both contain interrelated and interdependent contrasts. Synthesis is the answer to these two questions and many questions. But sometimes the answer to questions lies in the nullisis. Otherwise systems would be lifeless schemas, without alternative, development or invention.

Socially and politically speaking, when an either/or question is presented, one must always take into account the four possibilities of thesis, antithesis, synthesis and nullisis. Question the validity of the thesis. Question what is being heralded as an antithesis and if it is truly anti at all. Equally question how the thesis and antithesis are being presented as synthesized for frequently it is not a true mix, but a mere adjustment, a euphemism or exaggeration aimed at steering perspective. And especially question the aspect of nullisis for it not only means neither, it is the unlimited alternative.

The dialectic of large scale energy sources is currently typically limited to either the burning of fossil fuels or the ignition of nuclear fuels and both. Examples within the nullisis in this dialectic is solar power or wind and water power generation, harnessing geothermal energy (Japan is one of the most active geothermal places on the planet and one of the most ruined from nuclear experimentation) ocean current/tidal energy. The alternatives are unlimited, however petrol and nuclear maintain thee societal status quo. There is always more than one, its counter and the combination of the two, there is always nullisis, the unlimited alternative. Nullisis is the enigma wrapped in the riddle of the matrix of four, the philosophy of the duality of polarity.

The duality of polarity can be applied to the primary subject of questions and answers. There are right questions and wrong questions and there are right answers and wrong answers. Knowing there are such distinctions can lead to bettered questions and answers. The double meanings of the words right and wrong are both accurate in this intersection of ideas; righteous and correct, wrongful and incorrect. How are we different? This is an example of a wrong question. How are we similar? This would be its correct counterpart. The right answer to the right question is the distinct fourth part of this cross reference.

The significance of four resulting from the duality of polarity is universal in nature and traditional in human thinking. Some of the most untainted traditions and glaring examples of the universality of the matrix of four, the duality of polarity are held by American Indian cultures. Four is celebrated and frequently symbolic on multiple levels to American Indians in the Southern and Northern Hemispheres.

Four is celebrated because of the four seasons, derived from the duality of polarity of equinoxes and solstices, and the four cardinal directions, likely based on solar east west orientation and the crossing of this line with a north and south orientation. Though there are in fact many directions, in degrees, four is the basic number of directions denoted because four is just enough and not too much. There are actually many more base directions on further examination, there is south, north, east, west, the in-betweens, (northwest, etc.) up, down and inward and yet four is the base number for direction in American Indian cultures and all across the world. American Indian cultures observed four to be symbolic of completion and balance concerning many subjects.

So many American Indian groups utilize four in their creation stories and mythology that the cultural correlation alone hints at the matrix of four and the duality of polarity. One tribe and another neighboring tribe might celebrate different points in nature, one the coyote and the other the fox for instance, but four is more or less an embedded constant among most all tribes in stories and symbolism. Four is intrinsic to American Indian symbolism and the varying philosophies among tribes from Massachusetts to Seattle. Whether it is four brothers, four hunters, four arrows, four days, four years, four winds, four stones or attempting and performing an action four times, four is highly regarded. Ceremonies of various cultures are celebrated in fours as well; four days, four nights, four banquets, four logs or four phases. Many peoples, like the Cherokee, believed in one great creator, who was the only one who could make and take life and made all things in pairs of opposites, like day and night, dusk and dawn.

The Navajo observe four stages of life; birth/childhood, youth/growing, adulthood/aging, wisdom/death. The neighboring Hopi observe four stages of life as well, only slightly altered, as do many other American Indian tribes. On the other side of the globe the Hindus noted four stages of life too; student life, household life, retired life, renunciation. The Sioux and others observed that the heavens were made up of the sun, moon, planets and stars. Many tribes noted there are four parts to flora; the roots, stem, leaves and flowers. The Iroquois' democratic and humanist principles, some of which were adopted in the establishment of the U.S.A., are symbolically represented in The Great Tree of Peace. The white pine tree is depicted as having four roots spreading peace in all four directions.

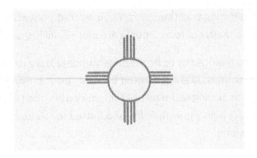

Perhaps none hold four as sacred as the Zia of New Mexico and Hopi of Arizona. They point to four as being a holy part of everything. The New Mexico State flag is composed of the Zia sun symbol celebrating four. All Zia celebrations from fasts to funerals are based on four. The Zia celebrate the number in recognizing the four seasons, four stages of life, the four stages of a day, four winds and four sacred obligations to one's physical, mental, spiritual and social health. Four is part of everything to the Zia and represents the four parts of man; heart, mind, body and spirit. The circle in the sacred Zia symbol represents the central true oneness, while the four sets of four lines represent four influencing everything on this Earthly plane.

The Hopi ancestral land is now located near the Four Corners area. The Hopi believe that we are living in the fourth age of the planet. They believe they arose from four levels underground just as the Zia, both sharing common ancestry. The Hopi also believe that there are four different brother creeds in the world, all equal brothers. The Hopi believe that people are colored akin to corn and that the great creator manifested people and corn together. The different types of corn have different attributes, but are all corn as people are all brothers the same.

According to the Hopi, there are red, yellow, purple and white people synonymous with the colors of corn. Each color is related to an element and anyone can potentially lose their way and become two-hearted. The term two-hearted comes from the Hopi concept that people originally have one heart and are good natured. People who lose the way, or lose self-consciousness, and succumb to greed acquire a whole other heart to feed, like working for an institution. According to Hopi belief, red people are the guardians of Earth, yellow people are the guardians of air, purple people are the guardians of water and white people are the guardians of fire.

People have been subdivided and grouped into numerous more races than four, though we are all human, we are all brothers. However for basic descriptive purposes four is enough of a distinction, for the only differences are shades, hues. People are the same only appearing in different hues of man. All of our differing traditions are all human traditions after all, practically all relatable as similar through thee matrix of four. People are more similar than different.

Racist divisional groupings are so nuanced as to be seemingly unnecessary to anything save serving unconscious us and them notions, likely generated by institutions seeking to control the dialectic. People should be proud of accomplishments of their ancestors and self, but being proud for being born a certain way is highly questionable and hatred for someone born a certain way is despicable in its ignorance alone.

The duality of polarity is apparent in the universe, human tradition, philosophy and even our very biological makeup. But these consistencies only point to its noteworthiness. The main significance of the multicultural traditional celebrations of the matrix of four and the duality of polarity point to the fact that we are all brothers mentally and spiritually. The matrix of four begins with assisting understanding as a cross reference system and as Occam's razor assisting understanding the totality of a subject or object. Its power grows through the thesis, antithesis, synthesis, nullisis set, the fourth part representing expanded and unlimited alternative. The political and social power of the matrix of four and the duality of polarity is in its deliberative ability to examine and understand the totality of a subject or object, even extremely complex ones, even those engrained into our very consciousness.

The duality of polarity can be applied to understanding one of the oldest and most complicated social and political problems; prejudice. And when one understand the totality of a problem one can fix it. Prejudice stems from the ongoing problem that has plagued humanity forever, the problem from which all woes and wars originate; an undeveloped or lost consciousness or as the Hopi would say, from having two-hearts. An undeveloped conscious can be steered by shadows and made to be convinced prejudiced thinking and being is somehow correct, however prejudiced thinking is systemic of undeveloped consciousness or worse, unconsciousness.

It is our nature to question. Only an undeveloped consciousness or someone who is unconscious would practice prejudice. Prejudgment of any object or subject, especially the prejudgment of another human as complex as we tend to be is not our nature. Prejudgment requires a level of certainty of unknowns, such certainty is the epitome of ignorance and the beginning of madness. One either has lost or never developed consciousness and moreover one loses humanity in prejudice and prejudgment, for one loses compassion for brothers and also loses or gives up the ability to independently question and answer. One already has certainty for an answer.

Prejudice is a form of limiting doublethink. The either/or mentality of separation is learned and nurtured, prejudice is not natural. No one is born prejudiced, prejudice is taught. People may be born with some sort of network in our mentality making it seem logical for people to place judgments and even understand things in us and them, but all people learn prejudices. It may be part of our unconscious lower thinking, but it is not necessarily a tribal inheritance, as many tribes historically welcome newcomers, like the Hopi and most all Native Americans, though certainly racism is primitive. People think in polarity so the us and them mentality of prejudice is easily instituted, but prejudiced thinking is not a natural inclination unless one considers lost consciousness a natural state. The only natural inclination of the us and them mentality might be primordially rooted in a disdain for wrongdoers. This tendency is socially nurtured and often manipulated to be aimed at some conjured grouping of perceived outsiders.

Prejudiced thinking comes from lost consciousness and from becoming, for all extents and purposes inhuman, two-hearted, practicing doublethink. Prejudice arrives in many particular forms postured at peoples sometimes from the same area who seem similar to outsiders in appearance and belief. Prejudice and racism go every which way and might be against one group of people or multiple groups, but no matter its form it is nonsense, as is every absolute prejudgment of every object or subject. The specifics of prejudice vary infinitely however through the duality of polarity there are four cardinal forms of prejudice amidst the many particular directions of ignorant preconception.

Prejudice of fellow human beings is based on four base subjects, the specifics of which are near limitless. The four categories of human prejudice are religious, institutional/national, cultural and racial. Mostly prejudice is simply based on the color of one's skin, or other inherited racial features, though sometimes it is much more nuanced and complicated than that. No matter the variations, human prejudice is based on these four categories.

These four categories form the set of prejudices people use to judge others. And with the duality of polarity the ways prejudice is implemented can be dissected and understood as well. Like the Yin Yang and so many other sets of the duality of polarity there is one larger, more common polarity and a second pair of opposites which is less obvious. Neither of these is more developed or distinct for all prejudiced behavior is foolish.

The most common prejudice is judging and acting against others because they are different. The equally common prejudice, the contrast of the first type, is judging and acting for others because they are similar. A less common and often overlooked type of prejudice is acting for others because they are different. And the last and equally uncommon part is acting against others because they are similar. Prejudice results in acting for or against others because of perceived differences or similarities, an us and them mentality. Neither of these is more developed or distinct.

One of the grandest problems on Earth is prejudiced thinking and being. And it can be extrapolated, dissected and better understood through the matrix of four, the philosophy of the duality of polarity. Prejudice is one of the oldest factors enabling exploitation and war, and it can be better understood and then bettered through the matrix of four. When a problem is understood it can be solved for it is confronted and problems confronted are halfway solved for as soon as one confronts a problem it begins to unravel.

Recognition of appearance is fine however judgment based on appearance is a show of ignorance and further an inability to question and learn. The Hopi conceived four different colors of people in relation to four different colors of corn and imagined people united as equal brothers, as one quad colored corncob. Prejudgment, especially based skin color, shows ignorance in a scientifically verifiable way, for only the human eye sees colors as humans do. Confirmation of differences in color is more confirmation of our intimate relationship, our brotherhood, for all other eyes on the planet see differently. No matter our hue, no matter our eye color, people optically sense the same. Whenever people point out differences in color they point out our similarity. We are more alike than different.

"All wars are civil wars, because all men are brothers." ~Francois Fenelon

"Polarity, or action and reaction, we meet in every part of nature; in darkness and light, in heat and cold, in the ebb and flow of waters, in male and female, in the inspiration and expiration of plants and animals; in the equation of quantity and quality in the fluids of the animal body; in the systole and diasystole of the human heart; in the centrifugal and centripetal gravity; in electricity, galvanism and chemical affinity." ~Ralph Waldo Emerson

There are four aspects of prejudiced thinking and being. None are more developed than the other for all circumvent questioning the present with past prejudiced answers. Contrastingly in Buddhism there are four aspects of love. Metta is loving kindness, Karuna is compassion for others, Mudita is the appreciation of the joy of others and Upeksha is loving equanimity for all things. Upeksha is boundless and free love and in its nature results in freedom to all who encounter it. The first step is love of self, then love of others, then love of others' happiness and finally true love for everyone and everything.

Politically termed the first stage is love of self. The second stage is love for all others within the collective no matter their differences. The third stage is love for all others in other collectives and cultures. The fourth stage is equal love for all people, places and things. Prejudiced thinking and being limits one to only barely knowing a part of the first stage of love.

In the book Your Planet Needs You, by Jon Symes four stages to living are described. And if humanity is going to develop we need to develop consideration of love and of the four stages of loving living, as presented by Buddha and in Your Planet Needs You; fair shares, living values, respect for Gaia and ever after thinking. These stages reflect the four stages of custodianship and guardianship through time as to having a bucket list.

One has to love self before being capable of loving others and one must love the joy for others before one can offer boundless true love for the joy to others and then all things. Love is like caring for the sapling of a tree so future generations can enjoy the fruit. The four aspects of love counter and alleviate the four aspects of prejudiced hatred just as a tree that bears fruit offsets future hunger. The fourth part is unlimited equal love and is the most developed part of the set of four aspects of love, while prejudiced hatred is symptomatic of lacking love for others, but firstly lacking love for self.

There are four aspects of prejudiced hate and four aspects of love. One has the choice to be either a giver or receiver of love or hate. One always has a choice, only sometimes it is difficult to see what the choices are. Frequently the solution to whatever problem there might be is love, or it would be. Often the solution is giving love and being capable of receiving it. Yet most, if not all of the world's institutions are all based on holding and taking. Most all of the world functions under the control of militaristic and materialistic authorities which basically coldly hate and coldly operate. Open hands and open hearts are the solution, not clenched fists and closed hearts.

The act of lovemaking itself is a physical expression of the duality of polarity. Meditative traditions, including tai chi and yoga refer to two intertwining lines of energy along one's spine being a third line which can be activated through meditation. The activation of these energies between two people in lovemaking expresses the duality of polarity when the two polarized and intertwined energies connect or more when two lovers hold hands.

Taoist and tai chi mediation practices describe activating energy and balance of self through the male and female energies along the spine, sometimes referred to as gold and silver cords accomplished through conscious breathing and meditative being. Meditative breath reflects the idea that individual consciousness is vertical. We draw breath downward and release it upward and our energy flows the same way. The stratum of mass consciousness on the other hand is everywhere, but it intersects with individual consciousness as a vertical line or field, at varying levels, because we experience things on different levels depending on our maturity or any number of things.

"Each one has to find his peace from within. And peace to be real must be unaffected by outside circumstances." ~Gandhi

Peace is attained by steady, aligned balance. The intersection of individual and mass consciousness forms a cross, representative of the duality of polarity and comes together in one single point. The world, mass consciousness, other people, might sway us, but not the more centered and balanced individuals. More grounded individuals are less likely to become upset by the swaying of mass consciousness. Normally those who are unaware of the four aspects of love are the ones who seek to disturb others, while those who are aware of the four aspects of love are less likely to seek to sway others balance. Individual balance is based on being near the center point of the intersection regardless of how one is pushed and pulled or otherwise sidetracked by outside mass consciousness. Individual balance is illustrated through the capability of maintaining alignment, maintaining the ability to be compassionate for instance, no matter how the external world, society or mass consciousness seeks to drag us down or move us around.

Balance and compassion in understanding love lead to empowered individual consciousness and eventual stronger interaction with mass consciousness. Just as there are four forms or levels of love there are also four levels of brain wave frequencies. Each is theorized as being more balanced and more insightful, more connected with self and capable of deeper connection with surroundings mass consciousness. Experiments in measuring brain wave frequencies found that meditative breath results in higher consciousness. There is beta (rapid), alpha (slow), theta (slower) and delta (slowest) states of mind. There is also a theorized gamma state that is faster oscillation rate than beta. The more relaxed states are perhaps more capable of giving and receiving love and consciousness. The slower frequencies, the more relaxed and peaceful states, can be achieved through meditation and love, as well as enhance love and meditation. Greater consciousness leads to enhanced learning and enhanced signification of learning.

The more relaxed one's mind state is the more capable of reaching higher levels of consciousness one becomes. This has been proven in experiments as well as suggested in meditation practices. The esoteric idea of the heart and mind connection, perhaps originally posited by Hindu and Taoist poets, has been recently scientifically validated as well. Relaxed meditative breathing enables higher mind states, enhanced consciousness and optimal being.

In Chinese the word heart and the word mind are the same sound, implying a distinct connection. One's right side is masculine and one's left side is feminine. When the heart and mind connection is open there is movement, release and ultimately balance. Balancing thoughts and feelings of the heart and mind leads to a heightened state of being. When the heart and mind are in sync and connected, when one is happy, compassionate, relaxed and yet aware, one's individual electromagnetic field functions at the highest optimal level. When one's electromagnetic field is vibrating optimally it is possible to influence and affect one's surroundings, via particles, waves, fields and outer mass consciousness. It's said when we essentially balance and then calm our emotions and thoughts, our true nature and true potential are realized.

"If the heart is light, the breathing is light, for every movement of the heart affects breath-energy. If breathing is light, the heart is light for every movement of breath-energy affects the heart. In order to steady the heart, one begins by taking care of the breath-energy...this is what is called maintenance of concentrated breath-energy." ~The Secret of The Golden Flower-Wilhelm

The heart and mind connection is symbolically shaped in the form of the duality of polarity, a connection of exchanging, much like symbolism expressed in Salomon's Knot, both flowing in out and out, both linked. Both the heart and mind are organs of real and immense power as well as more than symbolic influence and both are based on input and output. The heart takes in and pumps out blood while the mind takes in and pumps out thought. The connection and balance of thought and emotion lead to a balanced natural mind state, which in turn balances and integrates the physical state, resulting in heightened spiritual being. Balance of the mental state leads to integration with and balance of the physical, instigating an elevated sense of spiritual consciousness, heightened awareness of awareness. The meditation is secondary to the practice of meditation. Strong connection and exchange between the input and output of the heart and mind leads to bettered inner functions and heightened outer influences.

Scientific findings conclude people are capable of extraordinary feats when in tune with themselves and their surroundings. Our extraordinary potential is also validated by the oldest, most resonant and sacred esoteric symbolism, philosophy and theology. Science and theosophy prove that people have extraordinary capabilities. It turns out that independent cultures suggested the same things and not only through the dynamic of the matrix of four of course, but all hinted at meditation.

Some of the most intricate and mysterious esoteric symbols are intimately related through geometric symbolism. The Merkaba is one of the most intriguing symbols used for enhancing meditation and representing individuation. It is referred to as the vehicle or chariot of ascension. The word is made up of old Egyptian, combining three concepts, Mer means counter rotating fields of light, Ka means spirit and Ba means body.

The Merkaba is related to and depicted in the Flower of Life, a symbol used the world over, most notably in ancient Egypt, based on sacred geometry. The Flower of Life is seen as a circular and flat presentation, but is actually a flat portrayal of a three dimensional and circular Merkaba. Also within the Flower of Life is the Tree of Life. More complexly Metatron's Cube can be represented within the Flower and a torus. Metatron's cube begins with thirteen circles, twelve around one, to form what are known as the five Platonic Solids, by drawing connecting lines to points. The octahedron (two tetrahedrons, a Merkaba) is one of the five Platonic Solids. A torus is a lot like the symbolism behind the Merkaba, or three dimensional Star of David. A torus is a polarized electromagnetic field of input and output. The Merkaba and torus are based on the polarized exchange of energy from above and below, in and out, like the idea of the heart and mind connection and exchange.

The Merkaba is essentially a geometrical depiction of a torus. The torus electromagnetic field, based on the duality of polarity in the force of electromagnetism, is perhaps the most wondrous matrix of four there is. Everything in the universe has an electromagnetic field based on positive and negative points, like the Earth's the North and South Poles. And everything has inward and outward flows of energy, energy going in and out through the positive and the negative, like the ground and the atmosphere.

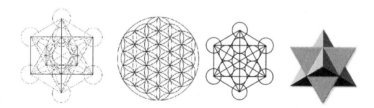

The Merkaba esoterically symbolizes the link of the heart and mind, the connection of spirit and body and of sky and earth producing lightning. Scientifically speaking the Merkaba is akin to one's electromagnetic field. Harnessing and balancing one's electromagnetic field enables one to be more influential on the electromagnetic field permeating and surrounding oneself.

The upward facing four sided pyramid (three faces and the base) spins to the left, and represents male and electric energy. The downward facing pyramid spins to the right and represents female and magnetic energy. The two tetrahedrons are perfectly aligned, only are in formation of the duality of polarity. As the two spin the upward electric tetrahedron points toward corresponding to when the downward magnetic tetrahedron points away. The symbolic depiction of the Merkaba is exactly depictive of the duality of polarity and the science of the torus is as well, a dualistic exchange of energy.

The Merkaba represents ascension of consciousness through alignment and balance of what are termed the fields of self. Meditation on building one's Merkaba or enhancing one's electromagnetic field/torus leads to enlightenment of self, individuation of the counter rotating spirit body, Mer-ka-ba, connection with spiritual and natural aspects. Meditation can lead to enlightened balance, optimal being and full potential as alluded to by the Merkaba.

One of the more well-known Merkaba meditations warns that it is important to perfect a set of three stages of meditation before proceeding with the fourth and final aspect of the meditation. Perhaps there is a secret specific form of meditation that supersedes all others. From what I have learned, the best way to meditate is different for everyone. Normally individually developed meditation in accordance to some guidelines, as opposed to following specific teachings and procedures of others, is the meditation of the highest order. Meditating on being grounded to the body of the earth and enlightened by the spirit of the sun is one guideline. Such meditation leads to optimal being. Practicing kindness too, leads to the same optimization and wellbeing.

One of the most healing concepts is made up of forgiveness and compassion and contains four aspects. This idea is both powerful as an inward and outward healing, as a meditation and kind practice. Each of these aspects alone is capable of squashing stress and confrontation, together quieting pain of self and others. The traditional Polynesian concept of ho'oponopono communicated healing concepts to better relationships. The idea was practiced by healers and is said to communicate something to the effect of, 'I'm sorry, please forgive me, thank you, I love you.' As a meditation the saying is a great stress reliever and as a practice can help solve problems and heal relations. I'm sorry, please, thank you and I love you are powerful independently and together can inspire healing inwardly and outwardly.

"If you want others to be happy, practice compassion. If you want to be happy, practice compassion." ~The Fourteenth Dalai Lama

Chapter 7

Right and Rule

"All sects are different, because they come from men, morality is everywhere the same; because it comes from God." ~Voltaire

The square is symbolic of order, man's ability to form and construct perfectly equal right angles. It is symbolic for fairness and equality. It is symbolic of the four Earthly directions and in many symbols, on one layer, it represents Earth itself. Both the circle and square can symbolize Earth. The square can be symbolic of the entire spherical Earth as interpreted and formed by man, squared away.

Laws and rules are such manipulated formations of man. Throughout recorded time laws have been authorized to control people, sometimes in prejudiced format, and to protect people from ourselves. Sometimes laws are fair and square and sometimes laws are exploitive, like blocks of a pyramid system. Many laws might be blatantly right or wrong, but wrong laws always pose as right. Legal and moral may align, but they definitely do not always align by any means. They are two different ideas and they intersect like lines in a cross. Wrongdoing may be conducted legally and righteousness may be done when breaking the law.

Legality and morality are extremely complex in and of themselves let alone the social and political complexities they pertain to. Everything is first biological, and everything else is political. And politics is composed of laws and the exchange thereof. The complexities of legality and morality have roots in politics and as such contain complex social equations equivalent to Einstein or Ramanujan equations. Yet the base from which the complexities of legality and morality extend can be understood through the matrix of four and the duality of polarity, through the dissection of the intersection of contrasts.

And yet first, what is morality? One must understand the separate lines before understanding their intersection. The measure of morality shifts in levels and degrees. Through the tolerance and intolerance of society the notion of morality sways. So what is the difference between right and wrong? A million philosophers, politicians, poets and prophets from Aristotle to Zoroaster and Mani to Mandela have questioned this most intense polarity, the subject most likely to be obscured and misconstrued, that of moral and immoral, good and evil. It is the most intense polarity in part because so many entities attempt to shade and distort the measure of moral and immoral in order to control objects and subjects in one way or another, often through a law.

Good is compassion and lacking compassion is evil, by degrees. And yet the concept of morality, of good and evil is polarized in our thinking much like our relative ideas of temperature. There is no real polarization of good and evil, the same as there is no real polarization of temperature. There is simply compassion, goodness, morality and its lacking by degrees just the same as there is heat and its lacking by degrees. Compassion and love equate to light and heat in this way. As well cold and evil are similar in that both are simply lacking. Evil is like cold space, lacking and without compassion.

Zoroaster was the prophet of Zoroastrianism which originates in what is now Iran in approximately 600 BC. Ahura Mazda is the god of truth and order, is wholly good and is the beginning and the end. Angra Mainyu is a contrasting spirit of falsehood and disorder and attempts to destroy the creation of truth and righteousness with the lie and the anti-creation. Zoroastrianism is based on the concept of a battle between the truth and the lack of truth, righteousness and nothingness, creation and decay. There is the creation and truth of Ahura Mazda, goodness. And then there is Angra Mainyu which is not exactly opposite, but detracting, for nothing can be opposite of god, just as nothing is opposite of goodness.

Mani was the prophet of Manichaeism, a popular Gnostic religion founded around 300 AD, also in what is now Iran. Mani's ideas concentrated on extrapolating and understanding the polarity of good and evil. He proposed good is made up of light, knowledge and asceticism, while evil is made up of darkness, ignorance and materialism. He posed that good and evil were in locked in an eternal struggle throughout the entire universe as well as in the minds of men. He proposed that everything existed in an infinite external and internal struggle between good and evil. Both Zoroastrianism and Manichaeism can both be interpreted as reflective of an external battle as well as an internal battle, a battle between consciousness and unconsciousness.

Of course Mani and Zoroaster were not the only ones to note this polarized struggle between good and evil, between the truth and the lie, consciousness and unconsciousness. The Egyptians presented this idea in their contrasting brother gods of Set and Osiris, one of darkness, the other of light. And like the story of Cain and Abel, Set kills Osiris, symbolic of the rising and setting sun. The concept of an eternal struggle between good and evil, the truth and the lie, light and dark is archetypal the world over whether explained in theology, philosophy or simply perceived. And resulting measures of morality transform politics.

There are millions of abstract and factual questions concerning the understanding of good and evil, right and wrong, compassion and its absence. And yet there is one simple way to understand good and evil without necessarily consulting the higher powers; understanding the Golden Rule. Do no harm. Do unto others as you would have them do unto you. This is a responsible notion which liberty itself is derived from. It is the peaceful way of live and let live. But because some people do not follow the Golden Rule, because some are either overtly immoral or irresponsible to the point or immorality, laws are instituted to protect fairness and steady the hold on the Golden Rule as much as possible, in theory, in purity. But in reality some laws are not parallel with the Golden Rule at all, some laws are far from moral.

In theory laws are instituted to control those who lose the internal battle of consciousness and unconsciousness and bring about evil externally as they seek to then battle for control of their external surroundings. In reality some laws are repressive of those who do no wrong whatsoever. Some laws are meant to disallow wrong while other laws authorize wrong. The polarity of legal and illegal is easy enough to discern. Rules and laws are written. Announcements are made on their implementation and removal. Lawyers are educated on the intricacies of legalese, court systems are set up with referenced decisions and perspectives. Whole forces of police seek out lawbreakers and elaborate prisons systems are constructed for those found guilty. However laws are frequently immoral and allow wrongdoing, often written by people who have lost said internal battle themselves and seek to control their surroundings. Laws are often immoral themselves.

Laws are authored according to regional tolerations and interpretations of what is right and what is wrong or presented to be in accordance with such. Sometimes, normally concerning the more complicated and lesser known laws, specifics are authored to keep a square deal for the few, to make right by a minority and not the majority. Some more extreme laws harm the majority for the benefit of a minority. Sometimes there is no correlation of right with legal and illegal with wrong as interpreted via the Golden Rule or by any other reasonable measure for that matter. Sometimes laws themselves are wrong, promote wrong and enable wrong.

Sometimes victimless crimes, actions which cause no harm to others are more frequently enforced than crimes with vast numbers of victims. Compare the enforcement of individual traffic laws with laws relative to institutional pollution. Some laws are written which enable and legalize great and broad wrong like the destruction of the elements of air and water. Some laws are written which criminalize harmless actions like protesting or jaywalking or otherwise being in an undesignated area at an inappropriate time. This stems from the unconscious seeking to exhibit more rule.

All laws are subject to measure of moral and immoral, using the Golden Rule as the center point and dividing line. Once that is determined the matrix of four can be utilized to cross reference the ideas of morality and legality. There are four types of law; moral laws which promote moral acts and moral laws which promote immoral acts, immoral laws which promote moral acts and immoral laws which promote immoral acts. Some laws instigate different actions by different individuals. Some laws instigate the crime they were explicitly written to prevent. Some laws are written with loopholes for the few to benefit. Some laws cease crime, others create crime. Moral laws resulting in moral acts are the distinct part of this set.

There are four actions relative to the intersection of morality and legality as well. There is the lawful/moral, unlawful/immoral, lawful/immoral, and unlawful/moral. The lawful/moral and the unlawful/immoral are the two most obvious and most commonly understood parts to the set. While the lawful/immoral and the unlawful/moral are the minor parts to the set, which might occur less frequently, but are certainly realized and considered less frequently. All individual and institutional actions can be interpreted through this example of matrix of four utilizing the Golden Rule as the centerpoint.

In this set of the duality of polarity, like so many others, there is one distinct part among them. It is reflective of the distinct and developed fourth part, the frequently omitted and unsaid part akin to Fear No Evil and the freed prisoner. The distinct fourth part of the set is unlawful/moral actions. This part of the set cares not what is written as law and is only concerned with the Golden Rule. The fourth part is the fearless civil-disobedient, the righteous rebel. Consideration of only the first two parts to this set, the lawful/moral and unlawful/immoral, actually makes it easier for exploitation to take place, often by those who consider the third part, the lawful/immoral. The fourth part is the most developed for it ensures morality despite the fluctuation of legality and proceeds basically on the path of the Golden Rule.

Most people behave in a lawful and moral manner most of the time. But some lose the internal struggle between good and evil, the eternal internal battle for self-control between consciousness and unconsciousness. They then act without conscious thought and harm others in an external struggle for control. External actions to take control, including instituting laws which harm the majority for the benefit of a minority, are arguably the result of unconscious people exhibiting external control.

People like to think that lawful and moral align and do not intersect, but they do. People like to think things are simple. Just as people would rather not consider the unknown knowns they would prefer to not think about the legal and moral intersection for they are complicated. Lawful and at the same time immoral legislation is everywhere among all forms of government. Any lawful march to war is immoral by one degree or another. Narcotics prohibition creates criminals and increases the contraband market and might itself entice users, but certainly entices criminal organizations. War anywhere and the war on drugs are always promoted as moral and good by some means, toward some end, but they are immoral however legal, however authorized. Immoral laws always pose as moral through some logic or another, and yet logic is fallible. And the more absolute logic is stated to be, the less reliable it becomes. Logic is flawed and ultimately leads to unsolvable paradoxes if questioned thoroughly. The certainty of marching to war is always an example of flawed logic with some flawed with a touted absolute at its core.

Some laws prevent wrongdoing, while others laws protect and institute it. Some laws are very specific and applicable to only a few individuals and institutions despite potentially concerning everyone. An example of such authorization is The Price Anderson Nuclear Industry Indemnity Act. It protects the nuclear industry from liability in case of fallout resulting from their subsidized businesses and makes nuclear power possible in the U.S.A. by essentially capping liability from any mishaps in their operations. Nuclear experimentation has destroyed vast sections of the Earth. And yet in the U.S.A. when there is a nuclear accident or disaster direct corporate responsibility would be limited and shifted from the responsible corporate institutions to the federal government and taxpayers. Nuclear experimentation taxes everything, biologically and politically. It is a matter of when and not if based on the logic of trends, which is one logical way of observing and understanding. Significant nuclear experimentation accidents and mishaps have occurred in the U.S.A. at Hanford, Santa Ana and Three Mile Island experimentation facilities. As well many nuclear power plants in the U.S.A. had their operating license extended beyond their original design specifications and as a result are constantly leaking 'harmless' amounts of radioactive material. Thanks to the Price Anderson Act we have nuclear power. Without it no insurance company in the world would sign a deal with a nuclear power plant. The government promotes nuclear experimentation.

Comparative laws are on the books which prohibit cultivation of marijuana and hemp plants while laws promote nuclear power plants, regularly polluting the surrounding environment and threatening everything and everyone with extreme blunders of hubris as well as the life threatening waste resulting in standard operating procedure. Marijuana and hemp are sources of fuel, food, clothing and shelter. Nuclear power boils water on a precipice and results in waste of unfathomable toxicity. The government prohibits marijuana and hemp cultivation.

The Supreme Court recently stated that corporations have the First Amendment rights that individuals do. Yet corporations do not have minds or mouths so they think in terms of and communicate with money. Corporations are now allowed to offer unlimited campaign financing. As protests around the world flared in 2011 the Governor of Wisconsin, Scott Walker, proposed a law that states protesters would be charged with the costs of police, cleanup and epairs and would have to file for a permit to gather at least three days beforehand, with the possibility they might have to prepay costs to qualify for the permit. Lawful immorality occurs frequently. Both these contrasts are of lawful/immoral acts, one directly for institutions the other directly against individuals.

Unlawful/moral actions occur everywhere, under all systems of state government. A plethora of examples are available in acts of civil disobedience worldwide. People commit crimes in protest for the good of the majority or an exploited minority all the time on the micro and macro levels. Civil disobedience, unlawful/moral actions, are frequently the result of an immoral law protecting institutional harming and harassment of innocents, like the lawful/immoral protection of the nuclear experimentation industry and the prohibition of marijuana/hemp and promotion of war.

There are many acts which are illegal, but are harmless, victimless crimes. The act of smoking marijuana is criminal and yet it is not wrong. The wrong concerning marijuana and more pecifically hemp, is that they are illegal. The war on drugs might have some logical roots, but ogic is fallible, and absolutism approaches madness. Infallible absolute manifestos, such as the prohibition of marijuana and hemp are especially fallible, for they are based on a proposed ocial absolute. Such rigid manifestos like hemp prohibition and nuclear experimentation originate from an internal certainty of idea, a perceived absolute nearing the sensibility of prejudice. Certainty and absolutism of an idea whether of promotion of nuclear experimentation or prohibition of marijuana/hemp prohibitions is said to be at the center of all madness. The more absolute one's presentation is, the more certain the dogma, the more mad ts originator is likely to be. Questioning certainty leads to invention, prejudgment and absolutism leads to madness.

There is always a better means to an end. Unless the intended end of the drug war is an enhanced prison system, then the system is functioning in line with its intention. The drug war as not solved social ills and serves only to steady the value of narcotics enticing desperate and greedy and build a police force to counter the increased numbers of criminals. Nuclear experimentation is meant to supply clean energy and yet its end result is a near permanently altered planet with wholly uninhabitable regions. The stated intentions for the prohibition of marijuana and hemp and for the promotion of nuclear experimentation, is to benefit society.

The status quo is maintained by laws and politicians who author and maintain the laws. Politicians, police and anyone else on the side of the law are not beyond breaking the law and when politicians or such institutional representatives are implicated in nefarious activities, they refer to the classic institutional slogan, stating something to the effect of, 'what I did was immoral, but not unlawful.' They insist this until they are found guilty of course. And in polarization to that familiar statement, when someone is accused of possession of marijuana or being in the wrong place at the wrong time according to an institution's interpretation, they are put in the position of having done something unlawful, but not immoral.

Laws are written to punish immoral acts and hopefully prevent them. But it is not that simple. There are some actions which have always been wrong and will always be wrong and should also always be illegal and yet there are protective authorizations. As well there are some actions which should never be illegal and only are illegal because they threaten the perpetuation of control instituted by some oligarchic laws in the first place. This occurs all over the world, no matter what specific form of government.

"When law and morality contradict each other, the citizen has the cruel alternative of either losing his moral sense or losing his respect for the law. These two evils are of equal consequence, and it would be difficult for a person to choose between them. The nature of law is to maintain justice. This is so much the case that, in the minds of the people, law and justice are one and the same thing. There is in all of us a strong disposition to believe that anything lawful is also legitimate. This belief is so widespread that many persons have erroneously held that things are "just" because law makes them so. Thus, in order to make plunder appear just and sacred to many consciences, it is only necessary for the law to decree and sanction it. Slavery, restrictions, and monopoly find defenders not only among those who profit from them, but also among those who suffer from them." ~Frederic Bastiat

Legality and morality intersect and like two intersecting lines form four points. Understanding the four points of legality and morality assists in measuring the actions of individuals and institutions. History encompasses all subjects, however political history, the history of civilization, of legal and moral, can be told as a story of individuals and institutions. In this sense there are four types of individuals as well as four types of institutions. Such relationships shift, but history as well as events of the present day, can be understood through this unfolding matrix of four, duality of polarity. There are individuals for individuals, individuals against individuals, individuals for institutions and individuals against institutions. As well there are institutions for institutions, institutions against institutions, institutions for individuals and institutions against individuals.

Practically every situation can be dissected and better understood utilizing the duality of polarity and the results of it. Sometimes polarity is simply the way the human mind interprets levels of objects and subjects. But many times the duality of polarity is a reasonably logical and even dialectically superior way to breakdown a subject or object to its most basic before deciding which direction to take in further examination. Understanding the intersection of legality and morality enhances social and political perspective. Equally enhancing to one's social and political perspective is an understanding of the differentiation of individuals and institutions.

Among many sets of four there is the distinct and developed one of the set. Socially and politically speaking the distinct one is the most developed and most righteous. The righteous aspect of the fourth part is another reason for institutions and individuals disdain for the fourth part. For those who would seek to control seek to control cannot control the fourth part. The fourth part is fearless, developed and righteous. And this aspect of four along with the unlimited alternative of nullisis, are the main reasons for the restriction of the duality of polarity and elimination of the fourth part. For just like the fourth part behind the veil of Maya in Aum and just like the freed prisoner and Fear No Evil there is one out of four which holds the most power and thus those seeking control and power seek to hide. The individual for individuals and the moral lawbreaker is the fourth part akin to the freed prisoner and the fourth monkey, the one those who seek to control would rather omit. When confronted with social and political options the moral lawbreaker and individual for individuals always utilizes nullisis in one way or another, toward something other than the presentation at hand, toward alternative. The fourth way is the way of righteous rebel, the individual for individuals, the moral lawbreaker, the freed prisoner, the unlimited alternative, the zero divided by zero, the nullisis.

"We are made in such a way that we can live in four states of consciousness, but such as we are we use only two: one when we are asleep, and the other when we are what we call 'awake' – that is to say in this present sate, when we can talk, listen, read and write and so on. But these are only two out of four possible states. The third state of consciousness is very strange. If people explain to us what the third state of consciousness is, we begin to think we have it. The third state can be called self-consciousness, and most people, if asked, say, 'Certainly we are conscious!' A sufficient time or repeated and frequent efforts of self-observation is necessary before we recognize the fact that we are not conscious; that we are conscious only potentially. If we are asked, we say, 'Yes, I am', and for that moment we are, but the next moment we cease to remember and are not conscious. So in the process of self-observation we realize that we are not in the third state of consciousness, that we live only in two. We live either in sleep or in the waking state which, in the system, is called relative consciousness. The fourth state, which is called objective consciousness, in inaccessible to us because it can only be reached through self-consciousness, that is, by becoming aware of oneself first, so that much later we may manage to reach the objective consciousness." ~P. D. Ouspensky, The Fourth Way

"Never let your sense of morals get in the way of doing what's right." ~Isaac Asimov

Chapter 8

A Set of Reactions

"Not everything that counts can be counted, and not everything that can be counted counts."

~Sign in Albert Einstein's Office

The duality of polarity assists in understanding the basis of subjects or objects. Most all of reality and theory can be examined through the duality of polarity, if it is not based on it already, to arrive at sensible and sometimes enlightening conclusions. It points to a relationship of multicultural relationships and is a mode of thinking, a philosophy toward examination and understanding of social and political situations. And ultimately, in the same intersectional form, the matrix of four and the duality of polarity can be utilized to gauge the mentality of individuals. And most importantly the matrix of four, the philosophy of the duality of polarity is revelatory of a way to better develop our full potential of thinking, our consciousness through realization of the distinction of the fourth part.

The matrix of four, the philosophy of the duality of polarity is practically everywhere, often mistaken for two or three and always as a contrast of oneness. The matrix of four, the philosophy of the duality of polarity expands thinking and being through nullisis. It enables exploration of subjects and objects in determination of their four cardinal directions.

The matrix of four has been practically eliminated from consideration out of a fear of four, a celebration of trinity, the instituting of doublethink and the craving for oneness without consciousness of its totality. It has been ostracized by those of the status quo like captors of the Allegory of the Cave. It has been nearly omitted because of its efficiency in extrapolation of subjects and objects up to and including the four cardinal directions of human consciousness. It has been overlooked as the ideal tool for slicing away the superfluous as well as understanding consciousness of self. It is quieted because of its social and political applications, but perhaps most significantly it has been nearly eliminated because of the unlimited alternative, the nullisis of the freed prisoner and the moral lawbreaker.

Man has a polarized mentality. It is possible that polarized mentality might be reasonable and yet it is possible to be unreasonable as well. Exploring unreasonable objects or subjects utilizing reason or the duality of polarity or any mode of thinking that might have some logical viability, is still unreasonable. The very notion of reason is subjectively measured in abstract, polarized extremes, but utilization of the duality of polarity toward objects and subjects that don't count is unreasonable. Consideration of objects and subjects that don't count, which are wrong to begin with, is as unreasonable as doublethink, no matter how much reason, math or logic is applied.

As animals we have instincts commonly perceived to be based on two main polarizations; fight or flight. And yet as people we can surpass these instinctual reactions. Fight or flight are not the only options when confronted with situations and circumstances where such instincts alight and there are certainly many ways to fight or take flight. The fight or flight options are frequently the only reactions noticed, but other parts are considered. The third instinctual reaction is fear driven also and is not necessarily exhibited less just noticed less. It is the freeze option. People frequently utilize the freeze option as well as Possums. The fourth option is noted as fawn. There are four basic animalistic instinctual reactions; fight, flight, freeze and fawn.

As beings of higher intellect we are capable of surpassing fear driven instinctual reactions, we are capable of higher thinking and being. In human dynamics these four reactions can result in varied specifics of fighting and taking flight. If there is a group acting out harm on others there are four ways to deal with them. Fight them or run away are the immediate options. The freeze option is not to become like an opossum, but to become like the group, to join those doing harm for self-preservation. The fourth fawn option is not to caress the tooth and claw, but to heal and teach the aggressive group and show them there is no reason to be harmful.

People polarize objects and subjects. It is schematic to our thinking. Perhaps we simply polarize objects and subjects because we have right and left hands. Perhaps people simply arrange things into sets of four, like instinctual reactions, simply because we have four fingers on each hand and four appendages. And maybe we have a numerical system based on ten because of ten digits on both our hands. It is arguable that one can find a lot of ways to put a lot of anomalies together and find relationships. One could attempt to elaborate on the physical and philosophical correlations of other numbers as with the matrix of four and the duality of polarity, but none would correlate with as many objects and subjects, no other number is so. No other number is like four. The distinction of four and the profundity of the duality of polarity are aroused from near magical and definitely mathematical instances in practically all things. The matrix of four, the philosophy of the duality of polarity provides base examination toward refined understanding on nearly any given subject or object, including consciousness, our thinking and being. The matrix of four is so ubiquitous as to be impossible to trace. It is possible however to see that people passively think in polarity and actively think using the duality of polarity.

Our thinking leads to our being, the internal results in the external. People are capable of creation and benevolence as well as destruction and violence, normally resulting from the most serious polarity, the internal battle for consciousness. Whether or not there is an eternal external struggle between good and evil, truth and lies, creation and destruction, gods and devils all across the universe is moot. This theological perspective may be accurate and may not be, but there is certainly such an internal battle within. It is an internal battle between the destructive and creative tendencies of the conscious and unconscious. The struggle for control between consciousness and unconsciousness is the eternal conundrum within. The internal battle for control results in similar external battles for control resulting in displays of our creative and destructive potentials. Whether or not any religious story is true they all provide insight. And the internal battle between good and evil and consciousness and unconsciousness is notably expressed in practically all theology as are the external results of the internal battle.

The truth of theology and sin is arguable, but there are some acts which are inarguably evil; exploitation, enslavement, murder, war, destruction of nature, all that which goes against the Golden Rule. Perhaps the Golden rule can, at least, in part, provide measure of reason as well. If decisions or some claimed logic or philosophy do not counter the Golden Rule they are, at least, more often than not, reasonable.

Whether or not the universe has always been locked in a battle of creation and destruction is unknown. However man has been locked in a battle of creation and destruction since time immemorial, this is obvious. History and current events show and prove this battle. Whatever the rhetorical specifics may be, the two opposites of creation and destruction have conducted and directed all of human history, both the reasonable and unreasonable.

People are capable of creating paintings, writing poetry, sharing food and building housing for others. And at the same time people are capable of killing numerous beings and destroying vast sections of reality in the name of one thing or another or nothing at all. No other species is as dichotomous. No other species is capable of arranging the destruction of entirety and construction of practically anything. No other species can turn everything into nothing and make nothing into anything.

No other species can accomplish or even consider the destruction and creation man may. People can formulate complex mechanisms of obliteration of entirety and equally complex formulas for artistic endeavors. The color wheel is a diagram of 12 and sometimes 24 dichotomous colors. The color wheel is based on normal human eyesight utilizing primary, secondary and tertiary colors in contrast beginning with red, green and blue.

Colors, as we know them, are based on our unique human eyesight. Colors might be interpreted as being light or dark in levels, and yet they are also dichotomous or contrasting. The color wheel is reflective of polarity in multiplicity. The subtleties of hues we see may seem near endless, but there are only so many colors the human eye can see. The decision making, thought process and individual reaction to information may seem as infinite as color, but just as people see in a certain spectrum people think in a contrasting and dichotomous spectrum as well based on the duality of polarity. People are capable of infinite nuanced thoughts, feelings and actions, but all can be interpreted as a set of four base reactions, four cardinal directions of reason, of thinking and being, reflective of duality of polarity.

There are four types of information based on the duality of polarity via the known and unknown and tangible and intangible intersections. As well there are four ways to interact with or react to information, four ways of thinking and being. These four forms of thinking and being are depicted by the four Wise Monkeys, the four characters in the Allegory of the Cave, the individual for individuals and the moral lawbreaker, as well as the first four characters of Genesis. This ultra-important set of four in the duality of polarity cross references reaction to information. One might ignore facts/act ignorantly, learn the facts/still act ignorant, learn facts/act malevolently and the learn facts/act benevolently.

Most likely, but not definitively, ignoring facts limits capability for righteous action. At the same time learning facts does not mean that one's actions will be righteous. These four cardinal reactions to information are the primary colors of thinking and being. Information might further be polarized as relevant or irrelevant, however to exemplify the figure as it relates socially and politically, information is considered to be relevant. Understanding this formation of the duality of polarity is a weapon of the highest order in the internal battle for control of consciousness and external battles for the same. It enables understanding of thinking and being and as so it's one of the most important extrapolations of the duality of polarity for it leads towards development of thinking and being of self.

The Wise Monkeys are depicted in relation to some sort of evil information, hence their titles; See No Evil, Hear No Evil, Speak No Evil and Fear No Evil. See No Evil ignores facts and acts without knowing. Hear No Evil learns the facts, acts ignorantly. Speak No Evil learns the facts and acts withholding information, representing malevolence. Fear No Evil accepts the facts and looks, listens and communicates information openly, representing benevolence.

Fear No Evil holds its abdomen, representative of withholding action. Inaction is often in and of itself a benevolent procedure. Inaction is also required for higher thinking, surpassing instinctual reactions and glimpsing intuition. Simply looking, listening and speaking are often benevolent themselves as well. Fear No Evil takes action, in inaction. The idea of doing without doing is a Taoist principle of thinking and being related to the fourth monkey. The idea is called

Wei Wu Wei and translates to action in inaction. It is not passivity. It is action without assertion, effective procedure with minimal effort. It is the polarity of the Tao, and yet in true polarized formation, it is considered non-dual action. Wei Wu Wei is passive action.

Fear No Evil, the fourth monkey, is often eliminated from the adage possibly because four is a homonym with death. It is also possible that observation of evil and open communication pertaining to the evil inspire those who benefit from or are accustomed to the evil to desire to be rid of the fourth monkey like those in the Allegory of the Cave wanted to be rid of the freed prisoner. The nullisis option is belittled and attacked by most institutions, scorned and mocked by most individuals and is the direction to developed thinking and being.

"Wu-Wei is the balance of minimal action and best result." ~Liu Xiaogan

The Allegory of the Cave is a description of the four cardinal directions of thinking and being in relation to the truth of the world and the lie of the controlling captors. The Allegory of the Cave is about learning real information and refusing the shadows of information, about being conscious instead of unconscious and realizing the objective instead of the subjective. The chained prisoner is forced to watch the information cast by the fire and takes it to be fact. The unchained prisoner is transfixed by the images, maintaining belief contrary to fact. The captors learn and accept the facts and exploit those ignorant of them, then correspondingly withhold information to maintain the ignorance. The freed prisoner accepts the facts and attempts to reveal truth and free the other prisoners. The captors want to eliminate the truth of the situation as well as the freed prisoner in order to maintain their assertive control. The chained and unchained, for various fear based and unconscious reasons, want to eliminate the truth the freed prisoner represents as well. The freed prisoner, the fourth part, threatens control, just as nullisis threatens control of any given dialectic.

The Allegory of the Cave and the Four Wise Monkeys subtly point to the ageless human predicament of the four cardinal velocities of thinking and being - ignore facts/act ignorantly, learn the facts/still act ignorant, learn facts/act malevolently and the learn facts/act benevolently - as do the first four characters in Genesis. This widely known matrix of four in the Garden of Eden represents the timeless thinking and being duality of as well as the distinction of one part. The first four characters in the Bible; God, Adam, Eve, and the Serpent are directly representative of the four cardinal velocities of thinking and being. The story focuses on information regarding the polarization of good and evil via the Tree of the Knowledge of Good and Evil.

The story, despite all its other allegorical attachments and layers, is directly reflective of the four cardinal velocities of thinking and being and further describes what happens when flawed direction is taken. The Tree of the Knowledge of Good and Evil can be reflective of many things, but it is directly reflective of information, knowledge. The Allegory of the Cave, the Four Wise Monkeys and the first four characters in Genesis all revolve around information, knowledge in general and specifically the knowledge of light and dark, good and evil, and the truth and the lie.

"To attain knowledge add things every day. To attain wisdom remove things every day." ~Lao Tzu

In Genesis the main lesson, quite often ignored, is one of hubris. Do not be hubristic. Do not act ignorantly and do not act as if ignorant of information for there are consequences. The story presents the idea there are many trees to eat from, many subjects and objects to explore, but there is one tree which bears consequential fruit which Adam and Eve are disallowed to eat from. In reality there is more than one tree, subject or object, from which stems deadly consequences, but the idea in the allegory is the same. And many such fruits share one glaring commonality with the idea of the Tree of the Knowledge of Good and Evil; hubris. An awareness of flawed thinking and procedure with plan despite knowing information suggesting one should stop, but convinced.

God warns that eating from the one tree will lead to consequences. The Serpent, with all the trappings of hubris says there will be no consequences. Eve is induced to be hubristic and convinces Adam to be so as well as they sought the power the tree was said to provide. Both are easily misled and seek power because neither questions reasonably. Adam acts blindly when two opposite sets of information are presented and chooses to believe the less consequential perspective. Eve is deaf to the warnings of God and believes what she wants to as well, the less consequential perspective. The Serpent knows the totality of the information, but acts malevolently to induce hubris, withholding information and lying. God revealed the truth and Adam and Eve did not accept his information because of a polar opposite presentation by the Serpent. And because the unconscious wants to believe there will be few if any consequences and great reward, they chose to believe the lies.

The first four characters of Genesis allegorically represent the four cardinal velocities of thinking and being, the duality of polarity relative to thinking and being. It describes man's ignorant tendencies, hubristic nature, conniving attributes and our ability to seek and distribute the truth. There are many other ways to look at aspects of Genesis, like all stories, allegories, adages and metaphors, it is layered and open for interpretation. The Garden of Eden and

Genesis can represent both the external Earth and the internal mind for instance. Refuting all the institutional baggage religious institutions have bestowed on the allegory for a moment, it is possible to see the Garden of Eden as internal and external allegory reflective of the duality of polarity of thinking and being.

The same ignorance, hubris and trickery, along with honesty, are evident externally, historically and today. The fruit of the Tree of the Knowledge of Good and Evil is the result of seizing power in a negative way. Whether it is opening the Pandora's Box of nuclear experimentation or taking power over another individual, ill results follow ill pursuits. The fruit of nuclear experimentation is death and lessened life. It is hubristic, and the external pursuits are based in the unconscious internally driven pursuit to take and hold power. Nuclear experimentation is a literal manifestation of Pandora's Box and as consequential as the fruit of the Tree of Knowledge of Good and Evil.

The genetic modification of plants for human use and consumption, to increase profit, is similarly hubristic, potentially diabolic and eerily relates to the Garden of Eden in seizing control over food and people through franchise operations. The genetic modification of plants is based on selling a franchise farming system of toxic pesticides, not feeding people. Whatever the situation, however broad or minute the scale, people behave with the blindness of Adam, the deafness of Eve, the deceit of the Serpent or the openness of God. People are either chained or unchained prisoners, captors or freed prisoners. And we are like the Wise Monkeys. And we are all capable of transitioning from one to the other like the Yin Yang.

The distinct one of the first four characters of Genesis is of course god. The duality of polarity and the distinct, special fourth part is commonly exemplified in physicality, theology, philosophy and deductive reasoning. Even in systems where there are simply two pairs of contrasts there is an element which distinguishes one among the other three, such as inhalation, or spring, or division. And if there is not one more developed of the four then one should supersede the equation entirely, like elevating to the set of love from the set of prejudiced hate.

I call the following the metaphor of the state. It pertains to four states with one distinct and more developed part of the set. It reflects the potential four states of war and peace in individual consciousness and collectives of mass consciousness. The four states can be applied to both internal states and external states, to both individuals and institutions.

Imagine four bordering states in a contentious region of the world. One state is of peace, is constantly at peace and prepares for peace. Another state is of war, is constantly at war and prepares for war. Another state is at war, prepares for war and yet is ready for peace. And the last state is at peace, prepares for peace and yet is ready for defense.

There are many ways the states may act and react, but eventually the warring state arrives at the border of the peaceful state. And the peaceful state will likely concede. The warring state will arrive at the border of the other nation of war and either they fight just enough to maintain the status quo or they fight until one loses all, while the other loses a lot. Now imagine the winning war state arriving at the border of the peaceful state that is ready for self-defense. Potentially the war state will decide it is not worth confrontation because of its strength or accommodation.

Any number of questions and quantifications can be applied using these four states. Which promotes institutions? Which promotes individuals? Which promotes war? Which promotes peace? This understanding can be applied to real individuals and institutions to understand the present and to make guesses as to the future. The fourth part of the set in the metaphor of the state, the most distinct and significant, is the peaceful state which promotes peace, but is ready for self-defense. One can imagine being in one of these states, both internally and externally, and quickly determine which is the more preferable mind state and nation state.

Perhaps there is, and always has been polarity and the duality of polarity as the most effective means towards balance or as the result of balance. Perhaps people do not seek polarity, but seek balance, and in balance is a required polarity. Expression of balance leads to points of polarity.

There a few absolutes in the universe. Mathematical and scientific absolutes can be used in understanding societal complexity, things that might seem unrelated might be neighboring extrapolations. A pinnacle universal absolute is that in balance is polarity, like a table on four legs. Balance is not only sought by human mentality, but is a primordial universal tendency exhibited in orbiting spheres. Understanding the matrix of four and the duality of polarity is one of the best ways to understand contrast and balance.

The matrix of four, the philosophy of the duality of polarity assists in building wisdom from knowledge, signification of fact. For only on realization of what is in balance can the point of balance be understood and sought.

There are four forms of lies whether originating from the state or elsewhere. The four types of lies are directly related to the four operations of arithmetic. Mathematical approaches can assist in making sense of the unpredictable dynamic of state interaction as well as making sense of and finding the truth. Institutions and their representatives, state or otherwise, constantly lie. Outright conjuration and total denial of fact are the obvious types. But the advanced lies are more nuanced and subtle as opposed to outright addition and total subtraction of information.

The first type of lie is addition of information. Sometimes the addition of a small bit of information can change the story entirely. The second type of lie is the subtraction of information. The removal of small key components can result in entirely different meaning. The third type of lie is multiplication of information. Exaggerations of situations connected with the story as well as exaggerations of extraneous information are included in the presentation to dilute it. The fourth type of lie is division of information. The facts are interlaced with disconnects and the significance of information is separated.

Understanding there are four types of lies perpetuated by individuals and institutions alike leads to more stability in your truth. There is less likelihood liars will succeed in lying to you or to others around you. There are four types of lies, however only one truth. The point of intersection, where nothing is added or subtracted, multiplied or divided, is the truth we try to be in line with and as close to as possible. Understanding what is being balanced leads one closer to that point of intersection, the truth.

"Deception is a state of mind and the mind of the state." ~James Jesus Angleton

Chapter 9

Life and Literature

"To be or not to be, that is the question." ~Shakespeare, Hamlet

Perhaps the most well-known quotation in English literature and one of the most well known in world literature is based on polarity or more specifically the ultimate polarity. To be or not be is not just any polarity. It is the polarity, the realest beginning and end. The Hamlet monologue goes on to contemplate the polarizations of life and death, the primordial balance, and the fear of it. To be or not to be, that is the question, that is the polarity.

Birth and death, the primal and ultimate coming and going, are polarized and yet related opposites. Of course there is a much more to the story, the in-betweens, but the human mind seeks polarizations in order to understand the balance. And to some the singular polarity is enough, but others question further seeking the in-betweens. The polarity of mortality, in birth and death, perhaps influences our thinking more than we realize, more than we are consciously aware of and is alone enough to incline people to polarize objects and subjects, even those which work by degrees. Perhaps people polarize objects and subjects simply because we face the ultimate polarity of mortality. But likely it is much more than that. Just as losing consciousness might come from fear of death, but it is much more than that. This great polarity is perhaps the largest director of polarized thinking as well as fearful thinking. And if one does not explore the subject and object of life, one might constantly be afraid of death, so afraid that one becomes unaware of the fear, and thus more subject to it.

There is much more to life than birth and death, to being and not being. And just as the Hindus and Native Americans note and celebrate four stages of life one should note four stages as well. Physically and naturally the four parts of one life are birth, puberty, childrearing and death. Mentally, physically there are four stages as well and without fear one might make one's own four parts. Life is what you make it and when one understands the ultimate duality of polarity, that of mortality, one understands the greatest fears of man, the end. With initial knowledge of mortality comes fear of death, but with knowledge of fear comes surpassing it.

Further understanding of death, as simply part of a greater spiritual cycle, offers alleviation of the potential fear. The Hindu culture long ago formulated four aims in life as well as four stages of postmortem enlightenment. The four aims are spiritual knowledge or dharma, wealth, pleasure, and moksha. Moksha is the postmortem enlightenment, sometimes equated with nirvana.

There are of course the four yogic paths to Moksha and its four levels. There is the path of knowledge, good deeds, devotion and meditation or Jnana Yoga, Bhakti Yoga, Raja Yoga, and Karma Yoga. The four levels of Muksha or Mukti are Ordinary Mukti; lacking consciousness of "I am God" or of duality, Videh Mukti; with consciousness of "I am God" and without consciousness of duality, Jivan Mukti with consciousness of "I am God" and with consciousness of duality, and Param Mukti; with simultaneous "I am God" consciousness and with duality and divinity in action.

The duality of polarity is everywhere at the basis and ultimate. However systems which work by degrees, such as temperature, are at the beginning and end of the extremes. The universe may be limitless for all extents and purposes, but there are only so many directions one can travel, temperature of the four forms of matter can only rise and fall so much, all solids, liquids, gases, and plasma and the void of space can likely only become so cold. There is one extreme to the limits of temperature, absolute zero, and there is likely no limit to heat.

There is no limit to heat just as there is no limit to compassion and goodness and yet people polarize hot and cold as well as good and evil in order to understand and explain relativity. One's actions or inactions might be compassionate or lacking by degrees. But as soon as the Golden Rule is broken, one crosses a line where one becomes immoral, where facades of logic become more translucent. As compassion becomes colder, by degrees, the appearance of logic dissipates. Within sets of degrees or levels there are points where things change if not physically than perceptively. The Golden Rule represents that dividing line between good and evil, while the freezing temperature of water might be noted as the point dividing hot and cold, relative to people. Matter can be only so cold, while there is no limit to heat. In the same way evil is lacking compassion and exists in nothingness, while there is no limit to compassion.

People tend to polarize whether relative to feelings or as a way of organizing systems into understandable parts, subjectively and objectively. The tendency to polarize objects and subjects, to contrast this with that, is a human condition. Realization of how we think and utilization of the duality of polarity leads to better understanding. When one does not understand this tendency and when one does not understand the duality of polarity and where it is applicable, one can be reduced to doublethink, unconsciously separating the whole instead of consciously contrasting the parts of the whole, unconsciously equating and misconstruing contradictions with contrasts and never knowing what's up or down or right and wrong.

"Our mind is capable of moving beyond the dividing lines we have drawn for it. Beyond the pairs of opposites in which the world consists, other, new insights, begin." ~Herman Hesse, Inside and Outside

There is polarity in practically all things and there is duality in practically all polarity and yet there is always more. There is figuratively always another matrix of four or matrix of more for that matter, an endless series of reflections and projections of subjects and objects. There is always more, but one ought to begin with an adequate understanding of right and wrong, as well as logic and illogic which the matrix of four provides.

Even if the present polarity is simply the beginning and the end of a group of levels and degrees, even if the polarity is based solely on subjective relativity of beginning and end points, there is obvious polarity in practically all things. Opposites do not necessarily equate, but they relate and help understand totality, not separate it. The opposite of daylight is not a chair.

Understanding the duality of polarity assists in understanding the basic and the esoteric. For so frequently the main polarity is often the only one noticed, the secondary polarity allows more complete understanding. Consideration of the matrix of four and the duality of polarity is not the only way to reach understanding of a subjects and objects, but it is a verified legitimate way. Many objects and subjects might only be sensibly polarized once, while others might be polarized many times and some not at all, yet frequently the duality of polarity equates to a basis for understanding that is just enough and not too much.

When someone proclaims there is good and bad or some other dichotomy, realize it is just not that simple. What is the perspective of this so called good and bad? No social or political situation is just black and white. There is, as the saying goes, the grey area. And in reality there are grey areas, the in-betweens or intersections of ideas which may be unlimited, but can normally be quantified into four states. Within any political and social dialectic there are always at least four choices; yes, no, mix, neither, otherwise known as thesis, antithesis, synthesis and nullisis. And no matter what the Golden Rule should be the unmovable midpoint that assists determining right and wrong.

Depending on the object or subject one or another option might be suitable. But it is always important to acquire new information when a problem arises. In this way the often omitted and disappeared fourth part, represented as nullisis, is special and should be pursued, for the fourth part is developed and develops alternative invention. Nullisis is the unlimited alternative, outside the cave thinking, new information to what is often a stale, static dynamic between thesis and antithesis. Sometimes we can be so caught up in such static predicaments that we do not adequately consider them and use flawed options because we have literally only conceptualized the thesis and antithesis dynamic.

There is a certain formula individuals and institutions use to predict and even steer the decision making of other individuals and institutions. It is referred to in contingency plans and actual events. It is noted in three parts and is related to the limited schema of thesis, antithesis and synthesis. It is most commonly referred to as problem, reaction, solution. These triads are equally limited and limiting, very much like the notion of mental, physical and spiritual; incomplete and unrealistic without natural. Without nullisis the concept of thesis, antithesis and synthesis is limiting for it only considers what is at hand and not what else can be, alternative possibilities. Problem, reaction, solution is the same limiting formation, so limiting it reduces people to predictable swarms, without alternative information. And yet only works when the majority is caught up in the either/or, us/them, thesis/antithesis polarization.

In these systems nullisis, the distinct and developed part, supersedes the predictability of the outcome. New information, the nullisis unlimited alternative basically eliminates the set of problem, reaction, solution dependent on the either/or mentality. Without new alternative information the triad systems of thesis, antithesis, synthesis and problem, reaction solution make it possible to predict social and political reactions to problems and have a solution for the problem prepared. However the prepared solution is often a solution which works for a few and solves the reaction of the many and not the problem which spurred the reaction in the first place. The missing fourth part subverts predictive constructs and limited dialectics. Some diabolical elements will go so far as to instigate problems in order to present such prepared solutions, new information and the unlimited alternative nullifies such predictability. Seeking new information is the reasonable and mostly absent fourth part to the set. It is the nullisis, the fourth part negating the immediate instinctual reactions of fight, flight, freeze and fawn and replacing the reaction with more calculated and thoughtful approaches.

When confronted with new problems, new information must be explored or new implementation of old information, not simply reactions based on perceived oppositions. The first consideration is which type of information should be examined; the unknown unknowns, the unknown knowns, the known knowns or the known unknowns. Different factors dictate one type of this set as being more useful to particular problem solving at different times, but new implementation is a constant. Realization of the duality of polarity as it concerns knowns and nullisis is a good starting point to investigate real solutions for problems.

The political system in the United States is a two party system of Republicans and Democrats. Frequently one presents a thesis and the other presents their antithesis, which is normally simply a variation or adjustment and not anti or opposite. Normally they debate and make compromises between the two ideas and create their version of synthesis. And yet there is always nullisis, neither, the unlimited alternative of new information.

There are many instances when one or another type of a set is preferable. When a new problem arises sometimes information we already have, perhaps applied in a new way will help. Other times, in many situations, new information is needed and the distinct part of the set is preferable, unknown unknowns. In many real and theoretical dialectics the unconsidered, the often omitted and the frequently eliminated is the one most likely to open understanding. One always has the power to examine situations and include the nullisis in any dialectic or debate as well.

Polarity is ubiquitous. The very basis of language is polarized, naturally and conceptually. In nature there is male and female. In language there is he and she, us and them, me and you, polarizations of verb forms along with the one we. The very basic structure of language is polarized. Poetry is notably often based on polarized quatrains, four lines, which contrast the sounds of language in rhyme schemes frequently set up as AAAA, AABB, and ABAB.

The distinction of verb forms and poetic quatrains are further indicative of the matrix of four and duality of polarity within our thinking and its influences on thinking. Since the duality of polarity is one way of critical thinking it is improvable. There are many systems of critical thinking and many systems lacking anything resembling higher thinking at all after being scrutinized. Understanding the ubiquity of polarity and the duality of polarity enables bettered thinking and new insights, but there are other ideas which are viable along with the duality of polarity or otherwise originated from its main power, the potential of nullisis. Understanding how we think opens up our thinking just as understanding the symbolism and mediation of information frees us of its unrecognized influences and rule. The duality of polarity is ultimately a rational philosophy, a legitimate mode of thinking because of the fact it is not an absolute. No matter the eloquence or authorship, no matter if philosophy or legality whenever systems of thinking and being claim social and political absolutes they are likely the qualitative equivalent of tissues.

Polarity is applied to systems appropriately and also inappropriately to systems which work on levels. It is variously instigated to divide understanding and utilized to contrast and complete understanding. Because polarization, even without knowledge of the duality of polarity, leads to some understanding it is implemented nearly automatically, only often in a limited fashion. If the in-betweens are not taken into account, if the duality polarity is unconsidered, if no nullisis is imagined, than any following notions are likely limited in scope, if not totally off base and a set up for the catch 22 of doublethink and some planned direction resulting from the accepted thesis and antithesis. People think in polarity and whether or not the presentations are inarguable like two plus two equals four or just shallow conceptions requires examination.

There is a myriad of human thinking and being. People are capable of destruction and creation and everything in between. Our destructive potential has increased to include totality, while our creativity is as endless as subject matter of the written word, our creative potential is frequently limited by demands and restrictions.

The velocity of thinking and being can be summarized into four cardinal directions -ignore facts/act without knowing, learn the facts/act ignoring them, learn facts/act malevolently, learn facts/act benevolently- based on an assimilations of the characteristics of Om, The Allegory of the Cave, Genesis, the Wise Monkeys and the multitudes of other multicultural correlations of understanding. And the written word, unlimited in specifics, as diverse as man, can also be categorized into four cardinal directions, four aspects based on the duality of polarity.

There are of course multiple ways to explore the concepts of written material however the primary polarity of literature is nonfiction and fiction. And just as two pages pulled from a book read as four pages of print, these two points become four as well. And just as the aspects of information swirl like the Yin Yang one transposing into the other and arising from the other, the four types of literature might seemingly amorphously combine or shift into four distinct directions or forms. The duality of polarity in literature is based on the subject matter as well as its origins; fiction or nonfiction based on reality or fantasy. There is fiction based primarily on fantasy, fiction based primarily on reality, nonfiction based on reality, and nonfiction based on fantasy.

Each of these formats is distinct and yet the majority of literature is variously a combination of these and primarily one of them also. Each cardinal direction is distinct and yet they mix. The subject matter for the written word may be near limitless, but all writing can be viewed in these terms. It is important to understand this about literature and moreover to understand this about life, because sometimes people lie or are so off base they might as well be liars. Sometimes what people claim to be based on reality is a fantasy and what they claim to be nonfiction is fiction. With the matrix of four and the duality of polarity one can better understand literature, the authored presentations of authorities and that most complex object and subject; our thinking and being.

The duality of polarity can be put to use in one's life socially and politically. There is never just one way of looking at things and there are never simply two ways, one being contrast to the other. There is practically always a third perspective and this nearly always opens the door for a fourth contrasting alternative, but no matter the numbers, there is always the nullisis, the nullisis spawned from the matrix of four. Authorities, whether intellectual or political, often seek to restrict thinking, perhaps unconsciously, perhaps as an unconscious action to take control. There is a plethora of alternative direction for thinking and being. Through nderstanding the concept of the matrix of four and the duality of polarity one can begin to see nlimited alternatives, the nullisis, in practically every subject and object.

Practically everything is polarized and people polarize practically everything else. And all too ften this is done to limit their thinking, often by their own egos. Whatever you do, however ou think, no matter what philosophy of mode of thinking you utilize, be open and expand. iterary art can be understood through the duality of polarity. Quality writing has active as pposed to passive sentence structure and equally quality living is active and not passive. Quality art and life is obtained through application of wisdom and method. The duality of polarity can be used to understand racism, morality, legality, literature and lies. Its cocooned ecret is in the unlimited alternative of nullisis. But its real ultimate power, its pinnacle pursuit, s in understanding individual mentality.

The origins of our creative and destructive potential can be explored actively by utilizing the duality of polarity. The first contemplation of the duality of polarity relative to objects and ubjects, even that of thinking and being, should always be if it is applicable at all and if so how. f not, if it is a system of levels where the duality of polarity is inapplicable, then other particular contemplations can proceed without hindrance of inaccurate and frequently misleading polarizations. If the duality of polarity can be accurately applied it is a tool as sharp as Occam's azor toward understanding if by only removing inaccurate perceptions.

The eternal internal battle for control of consciousness is a conductor of our tendency to polarize subjects and objects, even those which are best measured by degrees. The internal battle for control between consciousness and unconsciousness is enough to induce inaccurate passive polarization of systems which work by way of levels, doublethink, separating wholeness. This internal struggle for control between consciousness and unconsciousness usually stems from some fear or desire and results in external battles for control, confrontation, fights and wars. The duality of polarity initiates active contemplation of objects and subjects up to and ncluding self. And frequently just initiation of self contemplation alone is enough to win the battle for control of consciousness and realization of individuation.

Hegel presented this idea in the Master Slave, or Lordship and Bondage Dialectic. It is a dualistic thesis on the history of the development of internal human thinking and the external results of being. On one level it is a history of the world and on another a history of the development of consciousness. It describes two different entities, representing two cultures as well as two individuals as well as our inner selves. The more powerful entity seeks to enslave the other as master. It is a history told from through the window of history, from ancient Egypt to his own time. And it is a story retold a billion times just today, of the internal battle for control between unconsciousness and consciousness, we all face. Hegel correlates the history of the world with the story of our inner consciousness development, the micro and the macro, the inside and outside.

The story essentially goes like this: two entities meet and one enslaves the other. The master keeps the slave and the slave stays a slave, both remain unconscious and undeveloped. The master unconsciously takes control of the slave, losing self-consciousness. And the slave unconsciously yields to the master, losing self-consciousness. In the story, ultimately the slave fights for freedom and in doing so becomes self-conscious. The master has to deal with another individual as an equal and in doing so also becomes self-conscious. The four base stages of the Master Slave Dialectic is the first the master and the slave, pre and post confrontation. First the master enslaves and the slave surrenders, then each gains consciousness after the slave rebels.

The world is made up of the Masters and the Slaves, and also of the Worldlings and the Worldly. The Worldlings support and eat off of the Master/Slave system, while the Worldly support the Slaves and seek to instigate a slave revolt, in order to spark the development of consciousness of the Slaves and Masters both.

The unconscious asserts itself and takes control resulting in slavery to unconscious animalistic behaviors. Unconscious individuals ignore the Golden Rule and literally enslave others or and treat others inhumanely, frequently in the name of profit or structural support. Unconscious individuals who have lost the battle for consciousness assert themselves over other individuals externally. Conscious people will not enslave others, the only people who do so are those that lost the battle for consciousness. Unconscious people will do absurd, illogical, harmful actions for no valid reason, while other equally unconscious people will tolerate being under the thumb of such absurd harm. There is no logic behind acts which go against the Golden Rule. Whatever immorality is presented as necessity is the result of lost consciousness.

In the Master Slave Dialectic only after the slave fights for his freedom does he gain consciousness and after he fights back, if the slave or master wins and enslaves the other, there is the eventual and ultimate realization that such assertion and enslavement over another is unfulfilling. As soon as one fights for consciousness one achieves it, and as soon as one frees others one frees oneself. Simple confrontation or consideration of consciousness is enough to win over consciousness according the Master Slave dialectic.

"Until they become conscious they will never rebel, and until after they have rebelled they cannot become conscious." ~George Orwell, *1984*

Unconsciousness holds destructive potential in the desire to enslave inwardly and outwardly, while consciousness holds creative potential in the desire to set free. People unconsciously assert themselves over others and take control by any means necessary, leaving nothing off the table because they are unconscious. While people who have won the internal battle for consciousness uplift others and free them through deliberative peaceful procession, righteous rebellion, offering up everything on the table.

The internal battle for control between consciousness and unconsciousness results in external conflict and is another primal polarization, next to that of to be or not to be. To be conscious or not to be conscious. It is part of our condition. There is a battle within and being aware of the battle between consciousness and unconsciousness, between lower instincts and higher thinking, between the ego and the real you. Consciousness is initiated though peace, though self-actualization and in realization that taking power over another is unfulfilling. Only taking power over self and developing self-control is fulfilling. One can only cease the internal battle of the master and slave when one realizes it is taking place. As well one can only cease the external battle of the master and slave on Earth when one realizes where it originates, from the animalistic control of unconsciousness rather than the honed self realized developed conscious human being.

Knowing how to properly apply the duality of polarity and knowing when it is applicable to begin with, enhances understanding and potential. Four is special. The matrix of four and the duality of polarity operate as a way to understand sets of contrasts, which happen to include the basis of systems both inside and out. It offers a way to explore systems in the sacred four directions or extrapolation of related contrasts and it offers a system in and of itself to develop consciousness. Four is special and frequently the distinct and developed fourth point is omitted from discussion. The basis of orbit, arithmetic, breath and the ancient and predominant perspective on our very consciousness are all based on the matrix of four and the duality of polarity and give birth to it. Understanding it can lead to understanding consciousness and therefore an unlimited array of subjects and objects. The matrix of four and the duality of polarity, especially the distinction and development potential of nullisis, goes mostly unsaid. And the full potential of our consciousness is mostly undone and remains so except through piercing the veil of Maya as depicted in Aum, or as Ouspensky put it 'beginning and continuing to look for the objective consciousness' and as Schopenhauer and Jung declared 'actively initiating the developmental process of individuation.'

In correlation to the coming and going of objects throughout the universe and in the formation of the most reliable subject in the universe, that of mathematics, in correlation with our very breath and corresponding with the oldest and most powerful symbols, philosophies and theologies known to man, that of Aum, there are four forms of consciousness.

Consciousness and unconsciousness is just one pair of opposites, the second pairing is the subconscious and the supreme conscious. The fourth part, whatever one may choose to call it or even it is left unnamed, is the most distinct and developed part to the set.

Once the fourth part is recognized the subject or object in question might be more completely understood and developed on, including consciousness. Whether or not the duality of polarity is a conjuration of our thinking or an observance of physics is moot. It is both evident in the universality of physics as well as in the way people perceive. The matrix of four, the philosophy of the duality of polarity is not directly present in everything, nor is the function an absolute, but still, it assists in understanding and decoding practically everything. The matrix of four is not directly perceptible everywhere, but is at the basis of the most important subjects and objects as to be primordially important. The duality of polarity is not an absolute, just absolutely at the basis of so many important subjects and objects as to approach omnipresence.

Our very biological essence is rationed into a matrix of four, a duality of polarity. The spiraling double helix of our DNA is made of four base parts; A, C, G, T for nucleobase compound. The matrix of four, the duality of polarity is exhibited in the basis of our physicality and endlessly celebrated philosophically and theologically, and can endlessly be utilized to extrapolate the four sacred directions of infinite social and political situations. Ultimately it enhances the understanding of self and surroundings. And no matter the subject or object of literature or life, everything has a beginning and an end.

Chapter 10

The Matrix of Mind

Jesus said: If you bring forth what is within you, what you bring forth will save you. If you do not bring forth what is within you, what you do not bring forth will destroy you. ~Gospel of Thomas Verse 70

When I first 'finished' The Matrix of Four it very quickly became apparent that I was not done. Indeed, I came across so many realizations so frequently that I must have made three dozen major updates within the first year after releasing it. The seemingly endless amount of discoveries proved the never ending matrix like manner of the whole concept and astounded me at the same time. Each major new discovery led to new appreciation of the metaphilosophy and increased amazement of the dynamic wonder of it.

Because I am an independent author I was able to make the revisions at my leisure. If the work were controlled by a publisher, and if the publisher put up with including my new discoveries, which would not be, this would be at least the 64th edition. With inclusion of this chapter and all the other numerous revisions I made since first publishing, I officially declared a second edition. The information in the following chapter inspired me to make the revision and enhancement and announce that I put together the metaphilosophy anew.

As much as the book in hand focuses on information, the result of obtaining the information, for myself and for others, is often enough, inspiration. The ideas within inspire me daily. Comprehension of the metaphilosophy allows for reflection and revelation of consciousness spurring significant inspiration concerning development of thinking and being. So many of the sets of duality of polarity all notably spur inspiration and elevation of consciousness, and so many also suggest that within their construct of duality of polarity and four, is a pathway to impeccable understanding of self and surroundings. Frequently this is followed by the suggestion that understanding of the four elements of a set leads to enlightenment, and paradise, and even long life.

Knowledge of the 4 elements, of many sets, leads to notable advanced comprehension and as all the accompanying hints suggest, further subtle development too, access to higher thinking and being, to paradise of a conscious long life. The second edition spawned from exploring the 4 main dimensions of mind in yoga, each with four aspects, resulting in what is referred to as the 16 dimensions of mind. The 16 dimensions of mind are yet another modality used to enhance and illustrate thinking and being, based on the matrix of four.

It is said that meditation and contemplation on the 16 dimensions of mind, the matrix of mind, can lead to profound experiences of enhancement and enlightenment. For what it's worth, I can anecdotally verify the benefits of such contemplation. The benefits might be simply understanding from where 'your' thoughts originate and more profoundly enhances the thoughts one contemplates to begin with. The same can be said of utilizing any number of the sets of duality of polarity. Each set can be used as a matrix itself. For instance, meditation utilizing the Allegory of the Cave, a political and societal lesson, can lead to profound understanding, and of course contemplation of the Four PARDES in reference to any number of subjects, leads to dramatic expansion of understanding. Meditate on exiting caves of the mind. Meditate on pealing layers, like leaving caverns, to find the observer, or simply be the observer.

In order to understand the dimensions of mind let's contemplate yoga. The Bhagavad Gita states yoga is made up of four types of practice, all ultimately aimed at unification and balance of the heart and mind, of the physical and spiritual, of the four elements, of the individual and the universal. The four types of yoga are most commonly known as Bhakti; the yoga of action, Jnana; the yoga of wisdom, Karma; the yoga of devotion and Raja; the yoga of meditation. The four types of yoga lead to quieting the scattering static preventing the heart and mind connection. Each type of yoga works on, or works with, a certain aspect of our being so that we can develop ourselves. Bhakti yoga settles the ego, Jnana yoga feeds and calms the intellect, Karma yoga quiets the unconscious, and Raja yoga soothes our emotional side. Yoga clears our thinking and being enabling us to reach individuation, being ourselves, at our highest potential. The idea is that there are four types of paths to ascend; through body, mind, emotion, energy.

Yoga is further understood through the construct of the eight limbs of yoga. Physical positioning and correcting physical being are among the first stages to progress whereupon the more intangible practices, right thinking and right being, breathing and meditation are integrated. Yoga begins with the physical being and proceeds into thinking being, and then expands into the metaphysical, or spiritual. The inference is that when our body, mind, emotion and energy are united we are our most balanced and capable to expand our comprehension, expand our thinking and extend our being so as to connect with the universal.

Each of the eight legs offers immense understanding and practices toward self-development. Hindu and Buddhist ideas also demonstrate and elaborate on four base stages of meditation or our stages of absorption, called the four Dhayanas. The first Dhyana is reached when one releases passions and worldly desires for directed thought. The second Dhyana is reached when the chatter of the intellect is quieted and replaced with single pointed joy. In the third stage the joy fades and is replaced by total equanimity where there is neither pleasure nor pain. In the fourth stage all sensation stops, and only active equanimity remains and serenity of awareness and unification. Buddha then described four formless Dhayanas, attainments, or meditations done after the first four levels of meditation are reached. These are the meditation on the Dimension of Infinite Space, of Infinite Consciousness, of Nothingness, and the Dimension of Neither Consciousness nor Non-Consciousness. These formless Dhayanas are based on addressing habits and constructs, and this awareness enables them to be ferreted out.

Yoga (meaning union) and all forms of meditation assist in opening the heart and mind connection, and creating balance resulting in enhanced and optimal being. In symbolic terms thoughts are like fire while emotions are like water, in combination is steam and potential power. Yoga creates the steam, but yoga is much more than asana postures. Yoga will enhance alignment and balance, through the outer and inner steadiness required to stand on one foot or on your hands. Balance of the mind is obtained by practicing alignment of the mental and emotional perspectives. Physical work leads to direct clarity of physicality, and indirectly the mental/emotional inner world. In the same way inner work, as contemplation or meditation, leads to mental clarity and indirectly, clarity of physicality, and perhaps layers beyond.

According to the yogic philosophy and understanding of inner conscience, or manifest mind, (antahkarana) our whole inner knowing, our very thinking and being, is based on four aspects, each with four dimensions making for the 16 dimensions of mind. Correspondingly we have the distinct ability to comprehend and conceive creation through four main dimensions as well.

The first dimension of outer creation is the gross dimension, tula. This is the dimension we are capable of sensing with our basic physical senses. The second dimension is the subtle dimension, or sukshma. This represents physicality and actuality that is beyond our basic senses. The third dimension is asunya, emptiness and physicality of reality that is formless. The fourth dimension is Shiva, or that which is not.

These yogic understandings correspond at least in some manner to the Kabbalistic idea of Four Worlds, (Emanation, Creation, Formation, Action) four subtle layers to the spiritual light and grace that transmutes into the physicality we are, and we typically comprehend. Each of these levels of creation exists in more and more subtle levels. The more our consciousness develops the more we are capable of sensing these subtler levels of existence, and at the same time being able to sense the less subtle levels with more completeness and profoundness.

The more inwardly focused and present we become, the more we are aware of our own inner dynamics, the more capable we are of comprehending the outer world without exertion. Comprehension of the more subtle and finer aspects of creation is like insider knowledge. Finer attuned focus is comparable to knowing what goes on behind the scenes when most people simply enjoy the film, or like young children incapable of discernment of film from reality. The information is there, it is just a matter of knowing, or remembering.

The four main dimensions of mind include aspects of memory. We have knowledge memory, this is Buddhi. We have biological memory, this is Manas. And we have our individual memory which is Anahak. And in contrast there is lastly the Chitta, the universal memory or akashic. Each is made up of four dimensions for the 16 dimensions of mind. 16, or 4 x 4, is a highly symbolic number, of which geomancy, an intuitive predictive practice, is based on for example. And 16 x 4 = 64, or 4 cubed, is another significant symbolic number, specifically relating to consciousness, sacred geometry and the foundation of the I Ching just to start.

Each of these four dimensions of mind has four dimensions and each of these has multiple dimensions until there are 84,000 dimensions of mind. Perhaps these can be imagined as similar to 84,000 Socratic caverns, one can conceptualize and then breakthrough, 84,000 ways to witness the witness of self. 21,000 X 4 = 84,000, so each dimension of mind, ultimately has 21,000 dimensions, or each 16 dimensions has 5250 dimensions. This is tremendously complicated, but illustrative of just how complex and powerful we are.

84,000 is a highly valuable number in Buddhism and Hinduism resulting in the most profound and beautiful arithmetic equation conceivable, in my opinion, when the symbolism behind the number is realized. I explore the symbolism behind the numbers, in 108 Steps to Be in The Zone, but the simple arithmetic is 84,000 divided by 108 = 777.77777777777 ad infinutum...The whole concept of the four dimensions of one mind, and the four dimensions of each dimension, and so on to where there's ultimately the 84,000 dimensions of mind, all harken back to the primal idea behind the Yin Yang.

"As the Great Ultimate becomes differentiated, the Two Modes (yin and yang) appear. Yang descends and interacts with yin, and yin rises to interact with yang, and consequently the Four Forms (major and minor yin and yang) are constituted. Yin and yang interact and generate the Four Forms of Heaven: the element of weakness and the element of strength interact and generate the Four Forms of Earth; and consequently the Eight Elements (heaven, water, fire, thunder, wind, water in motion, mountain, and earth) are completed. The Eight Elements intermingle and generate the myriad things. Therefore the one is differentiated into the two,

two into four, four into eight, eight into sixteen, sixteen into thirty-two, and thirty-two into sixty-four." ~Shao Yong

These finer of increasing subtlety are gleamed through exploration of mind and help us develop more and more comprehensive and complete understandings of self and surroundings. Increased inner clarity due to a measure of righteousness, forgiveness and compassionate approach enhances our demonstrable capabilities and our intuition. When we are unhindered by the clutter stuck in certain segments of the mind we can detect at more refined levels. When the dimensions of mind are flowing and open the more clearly you sense things and the less you are likely to be confused, whether the realization of the confusion exists or not.

The 16 dimensions of mind are like wheels, and the potential 84,000 more subtle aspects are like bearings and gears to the magnificent clockwork of our consciousness machine. If a bearing is loose, if a gear is busted, a wheel may not spin, the machine may continue on without any noticed change in trajectory, but only with one or two wheels blown out. The intended destination may be reached, just not in an optimal manner and at great cost. If the gears are fastened correctly and the bearings made smooth, if you have all your wheels spinning with new tires, you operate at a higher vibration, you flow easily and swiftly. The same applies to the dimensions of mind, when everything is spinning smoothly thinking and being operates on and connects with aspects of higher levels. When we can synchronize and unite our thinking wheels we enhance our capabilities and excel more easily.

The first aspect of mind or more accurately consciousness is Manas for our physical, sensory receptive and intentional aspect of mind. Then there is Buddhi, for the intellect dimension. The third dimension is Ahanakara, for the ego aspect. And the fourth aspect of mind is Chitta is the intuitive mind, the quantum mind, the dynamic consciousness of, now and of timelessness. Buddhi correlates with the mental, mathematics for example. Anahakara correlates with the physical, breath for example. Manas correlates with the natural, the cyclical seasons for example. Chitta correlates with the spiritual, consciousness for example.

The Buddhi functions on data and learned knowledge. The Buddhi is the intellect, the discriminating and deciding aspect. The sharper one's Buddhi, the more ideas one can come up with based on the data given. This is how most worldly systems understand the overall intelligence of a particular individual, but Buddhi is the simplest functioning category of mind. On the subtlest level of Buddhi is in charge of discernment of creation and creator, and at its depths there is subtle and refined discrimination thinking, and pure consciousness itself. Buddhi is the finite observing the infinite that eventually ceases the discernment, seeking pure consciousness understanding the infinite is within the finite. Buddhi is often compared to being a knife and Anahkara being the hand that holds it. If we are not in control of Buddhi, and the other aspects of our mind, our knowledge, our knife will cut ourselves.

The four aspects of mind each contain their four dimensions and unite together in a circular flow so there is not necessarily one that is more significant than the others, nonetheless the Manas is referred to as the lower mind. It is lower because it is regarded as the feeling and emotional mind. And yet at the same time, Manas is the supervisor of our sensory mind acting as receiver and transmitter. The Manas is our sensory processing mind in charge of the five cognitive senses and what are called the five active expressions; eliminating, reproducing, moving, grasping and speaking. Manas is also the biological memory that imbues our system, of instinctual, cellular systems and beyond. Manas is considered a fragile aspect of the mind.

The Ahamkara is the ego, the I am aspect of the mind. The Ahamkara enables our self discernment and also the suffering of separation of ego as well. The Ahamkara is often called the I-maker. It is the original individuation and declaration before the facades and the masks we wear to interact with others and the world are adopted. The Ahamkara is a ferocious aspect of the mind that has to be tamed or it will reign instead of it ruling.

The Chitta is the mind of impressions. It is our bit of the cosmic and collective consciousness memory bank. Our own memories exist within this aspect as well as connection to the impressions of everything that is, ever was, and will be. The Chitta is the infinite flowing within, through and around the finite self. The Chitta is the most malleable aspect of the four. Enhancement through meditation, meditative movement and yoga of course creates more opportunity to connect and link with infinite consciousness eventually, not simply at the whim of basic, ego impressions.

How can we be more mindful, about our mind? It is like using a horse to tame the horse, but this is exactly what we have to do, tame our mind with our very mind. Now it took you so many years to become the way you are today, so many years for you to lose that bit of youthful exuberance and spark of childlike magic you thought you would never lose in your childhood, so it may take some time to regain the spark and continue toward enlightenment. Things take time, but just thinking on a thing assists it to become so.

Be patient with yourself and with others. Observe yourself and your own thinking and being and ask yourself 'why?' Why do think or behave this way? Soon enough, you develop, but remember there are so many dimensions of conscience to gain perspective from and access to that you can always develop more. The way to develop our mind to take control of our mind is through enhancing awareness of every aspect the dimensions of mind. Understanding our thinking and feeling clearly is key to regaining control of ourselves and enhancing ourselves.

Understanding requires alertness or mindfulness. According to Buddhist understandings there are four modalities of thinking, the four establishments or foundations of mindfulness. There is the mindfulness of the body, mindfulness of feelings or sensations, mindfulness of mind or consciousness, and mindfulness of dhammās. Dhammās specifically means the elements of Buddhist teachings, but essentially these spiritual teachings. Through observation of these subtle different aspects we can begin to understand the mind better and begin to control it, rather than be controlled by it. The observer becomes the director and controller, no longer controlled, unaware. The observer is more capable of response, instead of reactions.

In correspondence to the yogic Four Dimensions of Mind and the Buddhist Four Foundations of Mindfulness there is also sometimes considered to be Four Dimensions of Mindfulness among Buddhists. There is sati, the aspect for recollection awareness so that we are aware of our present state, it can be considered to be single pointed. There is sampajanna the aspect for the recollection of where we are going and where we are coming from, it can be considered to be linear. There is dhamma-vicaya the aspect for categorization of our experience in terms of some model or another on a comparable plane. And there is appamada for the aspect of mindfulness that is watchful and vigilant of self in reference to the entirety.

The Four Foundations of Mindfulness; mindfulness of body, feelings, mind and the contemplations of the mind, essentially focus on analytical meditations. The Buddhist teaching of Four Foundation of Mindfulness is, again, said to lead to enlightenment and expansion of conscious being on its own. Contemplation of the Four Dimensions of Mindfulness includes asking inner questions of the posture within concerning our body, feelings, mind and intersection with external influences. A wild simplification of the analyzation is below.

How is the physical? How is the breath?

Do I feel pleasant, neutral, unpleasant?

How is your state of mind?

How do the more complex Buddhist lessons (including Four Noble Truths, Four Thoughts, Four Immeasurables) contribute?

Depending on how our perspective is, depending on our overt thinking and being, we may receive things differently, and receive different things altogether, and therefore be able to transmit different things, differently. The level of one's conception is going to result in how and what one is able to potentiate. How deep on goes into meditation and if one begins to meditate at all, or how much assistance one offers to others and if one helps others at all, are dynamics to consider.

"Cowardice asks the question, 'Is it safe?' Expediency asks the question, 'Is it politic?' But conscience asks the question, 'Is it popular?' And there comes a time when one must take a position that is neither safe, nor politic, nor popular but because conscience tells one it is right." ~Martin Luther King Jr.

And when we have tamed the mustang of the mind, what then? What are we to do as spiritual beings? Well sadly, the trend we see among spiritual literature today is manifestation, how to get what you want. Well manifestation may not be a negative thing, but normally these manifestations are selfish wishes rather than something that encompasses individual and collective concerns. Normally manifestation intentions might be so juvenile, on a spiritual level, that there is no chance they will be fulfilled, for it's like a youngster asking for more from the parent. Eventually the parent must say, 'no.' If you are practicing manifestation without considering the collective, and without considering the whole point of any manifestation powers, that would be gaining an endowment that enables your enlightenment, then, well, perhaps, like a good parent of the spiritual nature, the chitta aspect and its dimensions, will not allow the manifestation.

Surely when manifesting consideration of the energies outside of us, the needs and wants of others for example might better enable the manifestation. After all if the universe knows that the manifestation is what the universe wants after all, then forces will yield.

In Japan, a traditional set of four, in the form of the duality of polarity, assists in manifesting wellbeing and a way of being that effects your powers and skill set in a positive manner, but also, it is said, is a contributing factor to a long and fruitful life. The idea is called Ikigai, meaning 'a reason for being' or 'a reason for getting up in the morning.' The idea that can be traced back to Okinawa area of Japan unites consideration of the individual's capabilities and wants with what the world needs that you might provide by way of what you are capable of. The idea of finding this centering fulfillment is perhaps best put forth in the following model of Ikigai and of the duality of polarity.

The beautiful elaborative illustration on the Ikigai principle resonates on deep and profound levels in its ideas and its presentation. Understanding your Ikigai, knowing your reason for being in this manner, is considered to be of integral importance to a long life and a pleasing livelihood. The cliché of the retiree in a Western nation soon passing away after retirement is due to a lacking invigorating Ikigai, or reason for getting up in the morning, that is not just about money but positivity. The cliché of the centenarian in an Eastern nation can be attributed to finding the Ikigai that motivates.

The Ikigai directly incorporates a process that heightens the combination of individual consciousness with the collective consciousness. In the formation of the duality of polarity that springs multiplicity from it and more importantly centrality and balance. This model can be used obviously for the Ikigai formula to advance your involvement in a proactive manner with the collective, and also as a model to analyze different modalities.

The Ikigai cross reference of what the world needs with your capabilities results in the most profound duality of polarity where multiplicity potentiates and correspondingly a focus and singularity is fathomed. The ability to produce multiples as well as singularity results in understanding possibilities better as well as potentially heightened focus.

The design outcome of the model is similar to the symbol known as the Seed of Life, which is the beginning bloom of the Flower of Life. The seed has seven circles intersecting and this model contains four. Though different this duality of polarity model is a seed on its own.

"Hands that give, also receive." ~Ecuadorian proverb

How do your qualities intersect with the needs of the world around you? What can you offer to the world that resonates in a way that not only elevates others, but yourself as well, in the process? The world is one where accomplishment is measured by way of productivity, no matter if that productivity is complacent to the destruction of the elements, no matter if the productivity hinders others. Consideration of Ikigai can assist transformation of this dynamic to one that is more sustainable for the individual and collective.

The Four Wisdoms for a harmonious society of Buddhism can also assist in balancing the connection of individual and collective interaction; generosity, tenderness, benevolence and empathy. We have to encompass some quantity of goodness in what we accomplish, if only to counter the destruction that has occurred in the past. Goodness can be measured and demonstrated in a simple manner. Imagine how much you build through our own productivity, instead of how much you were required to destroy to accomplish your goals. Imagine how many you assist through your own efforts to help yourself, instead of how many you will have to hinder in order to accomplish for yourself. Kindness and happiness are not mutually exclusive, but mutually interdependent. The same goes for generosity and plenty. It is completely possible to profit by being compassionate and open instead of authoritarian and punitive.

"At first people refuse to believe that a strange new thing can be done, then they begin to hope it can be done, then they see it can be done -then it is done and all the world wonders why it was not done centuries ago." ~Frances Hodgson Burnett

"Knowledge and ego are directly related. The more the knowledge, the lesser the ego. The less the knowledge, the greater the ego." ~Attributed to Albert Einstein

When we are caught up in reacting to the experiences we have among the collective we frequently can only demonstrate our qualities and capabilities in manners that elevate us without consideration of harmonizing interaction through ideas like Ikigai. The Ikigai teaching enables consideration and instead of reactions we can better at formulating responses. We become more powerful rather than predictable. Understanding is enabling. Instead of simply being caught up and going with the flow, we flow with the flow.

The Seed of Life has seven circles encompassed in one eighth circle. According to researcher Mark Passio, the circles each represent one aspect of the Seven Hermetic Principles, or Principles of Natural Law, and the secreted eighth principle is represented by the circle encompassing the entirety. The seven are as follows, in this particular order; mentalism, correspondence (as above, so below, the microcosm reflects the macrocosm), vibration, polarity (fourth in the set), rhythm, cause and effect, and gender.

According to Mark Passio, the secreted eighth principle is the caring generative principle. Understanding leads to the ability to create. This generative concept relates neatly to the eight directions or eight trigrams of Daoism. The Hermetic Principles and Daoism are epic wells of knowledge and wisdom, but essential among the many lessons is self-development and potentiation. The set of eight hermetic principles are each by themselves profound lessons of great depth and in one way or another many have the duality of polarity subtly integrated or overtly obvious.

The fourth principle of polarity contains obvious relationships with the duality of polarity, and the gender principle is another with the obvious concepts of feminine and masculine, in both the material and spiritual realms. The correspondence principle as well as the cause and effect principle both contain less obvious aspects of the duality of polarity, the relationship is there. Even in mentalism, the rule that states all is mind, harkens to mathematics and the four operations of arithmetic. The rhythm principle also is at its core the energy of a pendulum swinging back and forth in contrasting flow.

Despite the horrible authoritarian world, there is no matrix of control quite as daunting as that depicted in the film The Matrix. It may be that certain institutions would like such perversion, and in a lot of ways, a lot of people behave like cogs, batteries, and mechanical units in a machine, it seems possible there is such a technological matrix of which we are a part. The social and political sphere can appear allegorically like a matrix of control, but it's our own construct.

There is no outside technological matrix of control, although there certainly are authoritarian tendencies that inspire institutions to reach for such it seems, and certainly some whose influences operate right now in parallel mechanical rigidity, but there is no actual matrix of control. The matrix of control is within us, is us. The authoritarian world can certainly influence us, but we ourselves are potentially our own matrix of control.

You're in your matrix of control, it is you. Institutions certainly use this to their advantage and make modifications so as to influence you and even make people believe they are in control, but ultimately after streamlining situations, you are the matrix that controls you. In the same parallax modality of perspective, no one makes you feel a certain way, you decide. You are in control of you and how you feel, or rather your matrix is. The matrix of control is of your own manifestation, it is not a foreign entity, not a parasitic institutional mechanical construction, no matter how many such institutions exist and attempt to influence.

The matrix of control is our own psychological construction. It's certainly influenced by our experiences, with outside institutions and individuals, but we form it. The matrix of control we experience and relate to through the film The Matrix is something we make for ourselves, something we agree on, and conceptualize and adopt as a persona even, and when we are able to pierce the veil, when we able to see beyond the false images of the matrix of mind, often of our own creation, we are freed from the patterns we are captive to and live under.

Some of the unfolding apparatuses of the matrix of four are so intrinsically symbolically related, despite variation or divergences, that it is almost as if the story of the Tower of Babylon is equally a tale of the split of verbal language as it is the tale of a breakup of symbolic language. The language of symbolism is the language of God, or Tetragrammaton, meaning literally of course, four grammar. The duality of polarity is so frequently related by so many diverse cultures that it's as if there are different grammatical understandings of the same concept.

Why would four, or the duality of polarity, have anything to do with the language of God? Probably many reasons, but certainly one reason is the godliness that comes forth when we understand entirety, and the duality of polarity assists us in this manner. The potential to move beyond a problem when we can comprehend it is godly. The matrix of control that prevents us from accessing our true potential is based on the matrix of absolutes we started with, the four aspects of the microcosm and macrocosm, each an absolute of four parts.

There are the mental, physical, spiritual, and universal aspects represented in the macrocosm as absolutes of arithmetic, breath, orbit and AUM. Only the absolute of AUM is arguable, and yet inconceivable, and such is the spiritual aspect anyway; beyond traditional conceptuality. As represented in the microcosm these aspects can become both our captors as well as the key out.

Individually we are all born with certain biological structures and limitations. The physical aspects are incredibly difficult to comprehend and overcome, but realization that our very biology can take part in trapping us can free us. We are susceptible to hunger, lust, addiction, and even less harmless circumstances like gravity. No matter our sex, or our physical endowment or deformity we are susceptible to limitations of our bodies, even capable of falling into traps set by our very our senses. If we do not learn to discipline ourselves we do not overcome patterns caused by our abilities or disabilities of our very biology.

The mental matrix of control is most often set up by conditions and parameters we learn to accept. All of society, the religious, cultural or governmental norms we accept and copy, the thinking we believe is our own, and we believe is logical and founded are often enough actually just a set up to keep us in a certain framework. Our thoughts and emotions are determined by all sorts of factors, and we may be limited by frustration, depression or any number of short and long term problems of emotional and mental wellbeing. In Tibetan culture it is understood, or believe that emotions are simply thoughts that are cemented, humidity that coalesces into rain and settles into bodies of watery emotions. We might have thousands of thoughts in the same time span that we have just a handful of emotions.

Moreover, the social structures of our surroundings can heighten and interfere with our potential, and for all extents and purposes cause static in our thinking and feeling. The thinking patterns set by institutions and even informal procedures among collectives result in certain modalities of thinking pertaining to how we end up being. The more obvious matrixes of control are social and collective constructs.

The universal or natural matrix of control is descriptive of the elements of our surroundings and their influences. We are influenced and operate in our surroundings of space and time. Depending on the planetary cycles and depending on the season and area we are in, we are granted certain potentials and limitations. We are part of, dependent on, and subject to the elements. Just as the planets effect the ocean tides, just as the minerals and movement of water effects the quality of it for drinking, all elements great and distant, or small and within, are part of our present potential and limitation.

The spiritual matrix of control is mostly inconceivable and certainly intangible. Karma is basically the measure of cause and effect concerning subtle energies. Our level of spiritual comprehension can help us see different things and differently. Inexplicable spiritual energy is what causes certain people to have a certain energy and visualize things in ways which others do not. All things we note have spiritual origins or relationships. The astronomical understanding that the spheres influence the tides corresponds with the idea astronomical understanding that they also influence subtle energies of living beings.

The dynamic of the duality of polarity is Illustrated in this consideration. In one pairing are the biological and mental/emotional, and in the other pairing there are the astrological and astronomical. This concept is indicative of the close relationships of the pairs and revealing as to why the duality of polarity is often misconstrued as simply polarity.

When we have issues we can root them to these four constructs no matter how we or others interpret them. An injury is an obvious physical limitation, social zealotry of some form or exhibition of amplified emotional reaction are indicative of a mental/emotional limitations. The second pairing is more abstract to contemplate and yet we can all relate to being part of our environment and either in tune with or out of tune with our surroundings. We are either in tune with the seasons seen and unseen, or we are not.

Now, how do we break limiting patterns set upon ourselves in physical, mental, universal and spiritual terms? How do we move past the matrixes imposed on us? Well the grammar of four, the philosophy of the duality of polarity contains many formulae as it pertains to awareness of, and the slicing off of the extraneous, the superfluous matrixes bonding us. The four powers of the Sphinx is another powerful set of four that stands on its own as a set of significance and correlates with other sets discussed previously discussed.

The four powers of the Sphinx as proposed by occultists are to know, to will, to dare and to keep silent. Not so coincidentally these four archetypal powers are akin but opposite some of the more simpleton aspects of the idiot, zealot, elitist, and patriot archetypes, as well as the Four Wise Monkeys of See No Evil, Hear No Evil, Speak No Evil and Do/Fear No Evil. The best way to approach breaking the patterns is to make the unconscious conscious to bring awareness where there was unconscious habit before. Conscious contemplation of the righteous rebel, the conscious compassionate, breaks the imposed matrix of control.

"You are called to be king of air, water, earth and fire; but to reign over these four living creatures of symbolism, it is necessary to conquer and enchain them. He who aspires to be a sage and to know the Great Enigma of Nature must be the heir and despoiler of the sphinx: his the human head, in order to possess speech; his the eagle's wings, in order to scale the heights; his the bull's flanks, in order to furrow the depths; his the lion's talons, to make a way on the right and the left, before and behind." ~Eliphas Levi

In order to dare we must know; in order to will, we must dare; we must will to possess empire and to reign we must be silent." ~Eliphas Levi

Likely the most incredible part about overcoming an issue we might have is understanding its existence. Sometimes we know exactly what they are and sometimes they are hard to comprehend, ignored or denied. When we have blockages we maintain stoppages. When we then face stressors we return to the point of trauma for there has been no movement. We'll revert to whatever point was most traumatic, or to whatever level of psychological cognizance we held at the point in time here the blockage occurred. That is why it is very much like people are not even seeing actuality when they are unreasonably upset. They are reverting to the point of blockage.

We all change and develop in life if only through aging. If we understand what hinders our development we can remove the blockages and continue on the path of self-development. Daoist philosophy points to four phases of training or development. The first stage is as a martial artist (physical), second as a healer (mental), then as a scholar (universal), and then a priest (spiritual). No matter our position or focus there is always room for expansion.

Sentient beings are numberless; I vow to save them all.

Desires are inexhaustible; I vow to put an end to them.

The Dharmas are boundless; I vow to master them.

The Buddha's Way is unsurpassable; I vow to attain it.

~Four Bodhisattva Vows of Buddhism

The Final Chapter

"Monks, there are three things which are not practiced in secret, not openly. What are they?

The ways of women folk are secret, not open. Brahman (one of four Hindu classes) practice their chants in secret, not openly. Those of perverse views hold their views secretly not openly...

There are three things which shine forth for all to see, that are not hidden. What are they?

The disc of the moon shines forth for all to see; the disc of the sun does likewise. The Dhamma discipline (dharma/teachings of Buddha) of Tathagata shines forth for all to see." ~Pali Text, Gradual Sayings

The Pali Texts Society preserves and translates original Buddhist verses and teachings. In this parable three parts are presented as dichotomously open and secret sets. Sometimes the fourth part is not presented, sometimes it is implied yet absent and other times it may not be so unobvious it goes unconsidered. Sometimes it is implicitly hidden. Sometimes we look for the fourth contrast or the answer to a question outside ourselves, when in actuality we have the answer, we are the answer. The answer is our self. Sometimes, as in this parable, the fourth part, missing, elusive, and absent, is the self. To find self, one must look, to activate consciousness one must try and sometimes simply trying is all one has to do. To be aware of the sun, moon and truth is positive awareness, but only when the self is no longer hidden can one develop supreme consciousness and awareness.

Like all profound sentiments there are multiple layers to this idea. There is polarity in the sentiment in the hidden and unhidden practices. There is the unsaid fourth part to the equation which can be hidden and might yet become unhidden. Keeping one's views hidden is perverse for it is never bettered by other people's views and no instigation of self-consciousness occurs, while practicing openly leads to betterment of perspective. If one's perspective is open it usually is logical relative to the Golden Rule, if it is hidden than likely it goes against the Golden Rule.

The sun, moon and teachings of Buddha represent real objects and subjects. The same goes for the idea of self. Self is an object and subject, as well self can understand both concepts and incepts. When self is included in the triads of hidden and unhidden the duality of polarity is more apparent. The idea displays the duality of polarity, including the unsaid inference, and the universal penetration of balance. Sun and moon are in balance, so is good and bad, as well as the external truth and the internal truth of self. Balance is the intuitively recognized power coursing through the entire universe creating the same spiraling shapes, the same effect and results in the microcosm and macrocosm, like a solar system compared to an atom and like a galaxy compared to a storm.

The parable of dichotomous sets reveals the brilliance of theological texts, with or without the addition of the notion of self. The sun, moon, the teaching and the unsaid represent object, subject, concept and the unsaid incept. Knowing possibilities makes understanding and influencing possibilities possible. Knowledge of the unlimited alternative in the matrix of four assists in expansion and division of possibility, like the four points in four sided Mandalas and the inferred in-betweens. The matrix of four is like a grid or a Pomo basket weaving. The weaving grid is near perfect in its repetition and yet there is an occasional skip, or stutter, apparent anomalies in the matrix which point out another surrounding grid. It is a grid work which clicks and notches together like clockwork. The matrix of four and the duality of polarity spawn from and unto itself. From it, it is. There is such a matrix in each part of the matrix. One of great depth is presented in the Allegory of the Cave. It is initially representative of a mental and individual cave, then a political cave, then a societal cave, then a religious one, and can be posited as a spatial one, each pertaining to multiple layers, that can be examined until one feels it necessary to go outside and try to rip open the sky just to be sure. A similar matrix unfolds from the equinoxes and solstices and the duality of polarity of breath and in nullisis itself.

There are many arbitrary points to many numbers and some numerological references could contain elements which are simply relative reflections. There are correspondences of four which may not be relevant to the matrix, but this book is not about the four bases in baseball. I believe the ideas discussed and the metaphilosophy discussed determine within the duality of polarity is a projection, a projection such as described by Om, a projection of the unstruck sound.

The duality of polarity is the projection of absolutes, of orbit, arithmetic, breath and self. There are projections outward and inward, as well there are reflections outward and inward. The duality of polarity is a projection outward and inward, and is exemplified as a reflection outward and inward, it is a matrix. Consideration of these four aspects or four types of ideas when learning of presentation from others, be they individual authors or institutional authorities, can lead to important enlightenment relative to the truth. The more truth the presentation is made up of the more projections and less reflections it is based on. The more real and truthful the presentation, the broader are its potential applications as well. Consideration of these four parts is consideration of realness and without it one might lend significance to artificiality or worse remove significance from authenticity.

"We live in a world where there is more and more information, with less and less meaning. Consider three hypothesis..." ~Jean Baudrillard, Simulacra and Simulations.

The book Simulacra and Simulations is about reality and perceptions of reality, projections and reflections. Jean Baudrillard proposed three aspects in the following extrapolation on how people think lacking the obvious fourth part. His cross reference was done via meaningful information without signification, meaningless information without signification and information being made insignificant or meaningless via the abundance of information itself. The lacking fourth part is meaningful information which achieves signification. This missing fourth part corresponds with balance and the realization of self. The matrix of four and the duality of polarity present a way to make signification of not only information, but self.

Within the matrix of four and the duality of polarity is the distinct and developed fourth part; self-realization. The matrix of four and the duality of polarity result from balance and in balance. And in this world of controlling institutions, of harshness, of jingoistic training no matter your location, of insistence one identifies self with institutions be they church, state or corporation, one has to be a righteous rebel so as to initiate individuation, gain insight and inception, achieving signification of information and self. Perhaps there is nothing more powerful in the universe than balance and being in balance. The matrix of four and the philosophy of the duality of polarity is a result of the endless attraction to balance. Understanding balance, through the duality of polarity or by other means be they arise and realization of self is the key to signification of information. Buddha attained supreme consciousness only when realization of the signification of balance was achieved.

Buddha was born a prince and later became an aesthetic, refusing worldly pleasures for six years in his search for truth and enlightenment. Then one day he came to realization, his moment of signification of information. He was sitting along the river and heard a musician tell his student 'do not tighten the strings too tight or they will break and do not attach them too loose or they will not play.' It was in this moment in the story of Buddha that he understood the middle way, balance. He later stopped and meditated under a tree and attained enlightenment during a meditation which there are said to be four parts. The first watch of the meditation under the Bodhi tree was the recognition of past lives. The second watch was the realization that rebirth depends on karma. The third watch was the discovery of the interrelationship of all things and that there are no independent substances. The fourth watch of the meditation was the recognition of enlightenment and the great awakening of Buddha.

Correspondingly there are four stages of enlightenment in rebirth according to Buddhism; the stream enterer, once-returner, non-returner and the arahant or fully enlightened one. Each of these states renounces certain fears and desires and gains aspects of consciousness in order to elevate to the next level. Only after reaching the understanding of balance did Buddha achieve supreme consciousness and enlightenment. In order to understand balance one must understand what is being balanced, in the case of a music it is a balance between tense and limp, form and function, of man and machine.

The matrix of four, the philosophy of the duality of polarity assists in outward search for signification of information, for truth. No matter the external truth it assists in recognizing, it is more powerful when utilized for internal signification of information, for development of self-consciousness. The duality of polarity is like truth that cannot be hidden, like the truth projecting from the sun and from within oneself. The correlations of the theological, scientific, mathematical and philosophical aspects of the duality of polarity all represent external and internal truth. The duality of polarity might be criticized for including too much theology or too much of one theology and not enough of another. Perhaps to some it contains too muchAum and not enough Jesus, but my intention was not to please the religious or religious institutions or anything. To me the main value of theology is not in the external interpretations and presentations of god and godliness. The immediate value is in the search for the essence of humanity, our mutuality. And the main value of theology is in internal explorations and internal presentations of self. All religions contain prescription toward self-consciousness and self-realization, frequently through the matrix of four and the duality of polarity. The nullisis, the moral lawbreaker, the individual for individuals and the righteous rebel are all part of the distinction within the Matrix of Four and The Duality of Polarity, as is inward reflection of self.

Religions frequently glance over the suggestion that the answer is inside, that the answer is contained in self for religions promote the idea that one should look inside their institutions for answers, while the religions they host and prophets they adore predominantly teach the opposite. One should look inside self for answers. The idea of god is not only external, but internal. God or the energy of balance, or whatever name one would choose to apply is everywhere externally and internally and can be found easier looking inside oneself.

Traditionally there are four categories of university study; natural sciences, social sciences, humanities and fine arts. There are four stages of learnedness as well; there is obtainment of knowledge, signification of knowledge, verification of wisdom, and utilization of intuition. This flow of learnedness is like the expansion and contraction of breath or the Yin Yang, intake and output. When one is learned, and self-conscious one can project oneself onto the world and not simply reflect the world. When one is studied one can implement from within oneself. When one understands the macro and micro of the universe, one can effect it oneself.

The nature of the duality of polarity is to describe totality in the simplest terms possible. Peter Atkins points to the matrix of four and the duality of polarity in his book Four Laws That Drive the Universe and refers to them as laws 0 through 3. They are the concept of temperature, the conservation of energy, the increase in entropy and the unattainability of zero. The book covers thermodynamics, the transformation of physical energy.

The science relative to the presentation of the Four Laws That Drive the Universe formed in the duality of polarity with the contrasting ideas of conservation of energy and increase in entropy can be applied socially and politically to human dynamics as well. The projection of these four laws that drive the universe can be related to an extrapolation presented by socio-economic ideas. The universal laws described in the book, the energy of thermodynamics can be related and reflected in human dynamics.

Human dynamics is based on the same grid-like pattern projected by the laws that drive the physical universe, however instead of the duality of polarity being based on energy and temperature, the human dynamic is based on fear and a measure of love. People operate in contrasts of fear and love as well as energy and temperature. The four forces that drive the human verse could be reflected as concept of love, the conservation of courage, the increase in fear and the unattainability of absolute zero.

Of course this correlative is arguably a relative appropriation. Perhaps human dynamics is not measurable completely via the fear and love duality of polarity. The validity of this reflection is up to you. The matrix of four is part of the quantum mechanics of the universe, a grand and intricate fractal, a grid among a system of grids perhaps. The study of quantum physics investigates the functions of waves and particles of energy and matter. Quantum physics ultimately suggests that consciousness is the energy, the balance of the universe and further that conscious individuals are able to influence the consciousness with our own conscious intentions. What we intend or tend to inside can be the cause alone for outward effect.

This idea arrives from the uncertainty principle also known as the measurement problem, an accidental scientific demonstration of the influence of consciousness, not infiltration of metaphysical evangelism. Only when an observer seeks to measure an electron does a particle appear, prior to observation it is a wave. The conundrum led many to conclude the influences and relationships of consciousness and observation, inside and out. Some theories suggest that human consciousness is capable of influencing a small percentage of the billions of particles and waves in our immediate surroundings. And individuals of higher meditative consciousness can influence greater numbers of particles and waves while distance becomes less of a factor.

All the information on the matrix of four and the duality of polarity, all the correlations of projections and reflections can itself be explored via a set of four, a duality of polarity. Thomas Aquinas proposed there are four types of laws in the universe. These four types are a duality of polarity and the duality of polarity is in them all, a matrix, a series of projections and reflections. There are eternal laws, divine laws, natural laws and human laws. Eternal laws eventually diffuse into human laws. Human dynamics can be sufficiently understood in the same way as thermodynamics for the quantum mechanics, the exchange of particles and waves are the same.

The ethereal balance, consciousness, is everywhere, external and internal. And the truth of balance resulting in the matrix of four, the duality of polarity is expressed in universal laws, divine laws, natural laws and human laws. The duality of polarity projects from balance and is reflected in human laws as well as laws of being human. In other words the universal, divine and natural not only effect the laws man legislates, but also the laws, under which man operates physically, mentally, spiritually and naturally. Thomas Aquinas noted just and unjust human laws and of course there is just and unjust being as well. Operating clandestinely with perverse philosophies instead of operating openly is one contrast.

Money is a measure of wealth and interest. What one does for money and with money is a measure of one's interest as well as a measure of interest in just or toleration of unjust humanity. It is now commonly accepted among socio-economists that people are more motivated by fear of loss than desire for gains. Fear of loss and desire for gain are the two main parts to this duality of polarity human dynamics. The other two parts, fear of gain and desire for loss, are perhaps less logical and occur less frequently, however they are parts to the set.

Maybe one or the other part makes more sense than the others for a given individual at a particular time. Perhaps one or the other is more sensible at any given time. However instigation and perpetuation of fear and desire are used to manipulate people. In the case of this duality of polarity it is necessary to surpass it, to claim nullisis and move on, in balance, via the middle way. When the options at hand are based on contrasts like fear and desire then like in Hegel's Master Slave Dialectic, one must make a stand for an alternative and in the process become conscious. One could operate simply in the duality of polarity of fear or desire of and for gains and losses, but no leader would. Masters and slaves in a cave would live in this dialectic. To attain consciousness, self-realization, individuation, golden mind one must make a stand beyond the duality of polarity of fear and desire of and for gains and losses. To attain consciousness and be a great leader, even if one leads only oneself, one must renounce the human dynamic of fear and desire. To be conscious one must lead oneself, one must declare that just should be done or one must openly declare refusal to be unjust any longer.

Leaders tend to have a highly developed intuition able to creatively construct. However leaders themselves develop their intuition and even Buddha built realization and learnedness through a process of signification of information. Some of the greatest leaders held no title and in fact were often know as rabble-rousers. Buddha and Jesus were two of the greatest leaders and their stories represent the greatest righteous rebels ever, leading thousands of years later.

To be a leader use the advice and information that other great leaders have left behind. But a more important prerequisite to being a leader is to renounce fear and desire and be a righteous rebel. When one is learned and one renounces fear and desire one can more surely and swiftly recognize truth and utilize it. Recognizing the truth, signification of information, becomes like recognizing the sun or moon. Leaders frequently adopt or use the ideas and words of others. Quotation or following great leaders does not make one less of a leader and such alignment does not make one a better leader. It is implementation of such ideas that makes one a leader, for the words of Buddha and the like, the ideas behind Aum and the like, contain truth and can be utilized. And recognition and capability to utilize truth for just purposes defines a leader.

To be a leader, to instigate consciousness, one can always begin by casting off fear and desire of and for gains and losses. One can always utilize the words and ideas of others and still be a leader. In fact one might lead more successfully, as long as one casts off the fetters of fear and desire.

I choose to follow in the path of those who were powerful examples of individuation, higher consciousness, individuals for individuals and moral lawbreakers. I respect devote people as well as devout ideas, but be sure my reverence for ideas of prophets does not equate to a reverence for the authority of the vast majority of institutions built up around prophets. Leaders make stands like that. One ought to follow the ideas of others of individuation, others who extract and present truth, others who find self-signification, but firstly an unfettering of the grip of the human dynamic of fear and desire of and for gains and losses is necessary to lead.

Fear and desire of and for gains and losses is a human dynamic that we are all accustomed to and its depiction through the duality of polarity is recognizable and yet it does not make sense. It can be explained and explored utilizing the duality of polarity and it is obviously frequently so, yet it could be bettered, for none of those states are developed or balanced whatsoever. Fear and desire of and four gains and losses presents no distinct and developed part. In it there is no balance, no development or realization of self-consciousness, self-determination or intuition.

Socially and politically one must look within, to oneself when balance is thwarted, for balance. One must learn to reveal the obfuscation of truth, hidden practices and perverse philosophies. For those who would attempt to hide information on the sun, moon and truth would certainly also try to hide or control the truth of self-realization and the signification of balanced leadership potential within self. And the omitted or hidden self-realization is often harder to calculate than the positioning of the sun or moon and can be hidden for the longest period of time. Leaders follow those of individuation for their ideas are recognizable as truth, like being under the sun or moon. Leaders follow the truth as interpreted and presented by other leaders and are still themselves leaders, for they actualize the truth from within.

Joseph M. Marshall III penned The Power of Four, Leadership Lessons of Crazy Horse. He presents four points on leadership; know yourself, know your friends, know you enemies and lead the way. His tone is one of individuation, pointing out that character is reason for leadership roles, not position of authority or hold on power. His set of four is formed in the duality of polarity, complete with the distinct fourth part.

Don Miguel Ruiz wrote The Four Agreements: A Practical guide to Personal Freedom, describing a set of four thoughts and actions toward self-realization and individuation. The four agreements not only inspire self-consciousness, but are equally great points of advice on leadership. Be impeccable with your word. Don't take anything personally. Don't make assumptions. Always do your best. He notes that our mind is programmed, frequently by people and systems who would assumedly hide the sun, moon, truth and signification of self in order to control. His four agreements are a set formed in the duality of polarity, with the fourth distinct and unique.

The duality of polarity is a philosophical tool toward understanding all four forms of information, no matter how one describes the set and toward individuation through nullisis. The matrix of four and the duality of polarity resonate throughout the universe, throughout the world and within us. It is projected and reflected and pertains to universal truths as well as personal truths.

There is much more to the duality of polarity, just as there is much more to the ideas presented and included within this book. Many of the ideas presented are but brief outline, with deeper, layered meaning, presented to demonstrate their correlative qualities as far as the relevance to the matrix of four, the duality of polarity. Such points are worthy of more inspection.

As far as numerological symbolism, the attribution of qualities to quantities, it is often rooted in some real representation, as in that of the four seasons being demonstrative of the duality of polarity. There are other numbers which might be relevant and correlative among a broad range of objects and subjects, but perhaps none concerning consciousness as four.

The most common form of numerology involves adding and simplifying the digits. 1 means 1 of course. Two or more numbers, 11, for instance equates to and simplifies to 2, the numbers are added up to make a simplified related number. The only way four whole numbers can result to four using this system is 1111, of course. The time 11:11, equating and reducing to 4, is known to be a moment of potential and specifically opportunity for peaceful victory. 11:11 represents an opportunity in time to be everything the righteous rebel embodies, peacefully elevating individual and mass consciousness. World War One officially ended on 11/11 at 11:11 AM, 1918. The victory or peace sign made with two fingers, an eleven is exemplary of the concept, of peace/victory/eleven.

Another interesting and seeming coincidence about 11, the number itself of coincidence of time, is that on 11/11/2011 there was 1 year, 1, month and 11 days until December 22, 2012. The 21st being a day of great fascination and poignancy because of the highly auspicious ending of the Mayan calendar, possibly random, but interesting coincidence concerning the auspicious point in time.

The transformation of thinking into being, of thought into action can be represented in four parts. Knowledge is external facts. Wisdom is understanding of the facts. Intuition is knowledge and wisdom combined to make deductions from within. And the fourth part is leadership. One must learn knowledge to gain wisdom and initiate intuition, only then can one qualifiedly lead.

"Intuition is the only real thing valuable." ~Albert Einstein

I took on this project understanding that correlating political philosophy with divinity and science with spirituality is controversial. However my intention and the underlying concept of the duality of polarity is one of unification, not automatic respect for authority, be it political, corporate or religious. The duality of polarity correlates what some presumed were contentious subjects and objects. Religious detractors and detractors of religion seek to separate, the duality of polarity is of unification. The difference between the duality of polarity and theosophical and political dogma is that the duality of polarity is inclusive whereas politics and religion results in variations of us and them beliefs, which should be unacceptable to anyone at any time, leader or otherwise.

Leaders do not equate to masters, like in Hegel's Master Slave Dialectic. Leaders more often than not make a stand for individuals who might not be in a position to make a stand themselves, people allegorically akin to slaves, near voiceless and near powerless. And leaders make such stands despite opposition from authorities, allegorically akin to masters. Leaders do this like Jesus in the temple, like Socrates in the streets and on and on to the likes of Joseph M. Marshall III pointing out the importance of character not power.

The unlimited alternative, the distinction of four, nullisis, the righteous rebel, supreme consciousness, intuition, equal love for all, realization, quality being and leadership are all examples of the distinction of fourth part. The duality of polarity is like the golden ratio, apparent in practically all subjects, objects, concepts and incepts for thousands of years. The matrix of four, the philosophy of the duality of polarity is a tool to develop consciousness and loving compassion.

"If you are not willing to learn, no one can help you.

If you are determined to learn, no one can stop you."

~Unknown

Another series of reflections of the matrix of four, the philosophy of the duality of polarity was expressed by Arthur Young, an inventor and philosopher. He authored the Geometry of Meaning and The Reflexive Universe, The Evolution of Consciousness. He proposed reality is a fourfold structure, correlates the idea with multiple traditions as well as mathematical systems. There is the point-like (fire, no space and no time) linear (water, time-like), planar (air, space-like), and solid (earth, time and space).

He further proposed that evolution of the universe was a seven stage system as reflected in seven levels of evolutionary being. Light transforms into particles, then atoms, molecules, plants, animals and finally consciousness as in human consciousness. Arthur Young also theorized a fourfold matrix of the learning process. First there is unconscious action as if reaching for fire, then unconscious reaction as if feeling its heat and pulling away. This is followed by unconscious reaction to avoid fire and being burned in the future. And finally conscious action utilizing and mastering fire as a tool. Learning itself is a four stage transformational process based on the matrix of four and the philosophy of the duality of polarity. Keep learning, keep thinking and one can transform unconscious action into conscious action.

"God sleeps in the minerals, awakens in plants, walks in animals, and thinks in man."

~Arthur Young

"Live as if you were to die tomorrow. Learn as if you were to live forever."

~Gandhi

Another beautiful elaboration on the four stages of learning is called the Conscious Competence Learning Matrix. Frequently referred to in psychological circles as well as in business development programs, this matrix of learning is extremely valuable, especially when combined with understanding of Arthur Young's model. First there is unconscious incompetence, total inability. Next is conscious incompetence, realization of one's inability, then conscious competence or limited ability and finally unconscious competence or profound ability. In learning one goes from having no clue to being capable of performing the task, refining it and doing it in combination with other tasks.

The matrix of conscious competence is often confused with what is known as the Johari Window, both being utilized together. Joseph Luft and Harry Ingram invented the concept of the Johari Window in 1955. It assists the understanding of our relationships, of interpersonal exchange. The Johari Window depicts and describes four quadrants of perspective based on the philosophy of the duality of polarity. The first idea of intersection is that of self and others. The second idea is of known and not known. This intersection of ideas results in four different rooms of relationships; the arena -what you and others know, the blind spot -what others know and you do not know, the facade -what neither party consciously knows and the unknown what you know and they don't.

Learning how to learn betters our understanding of the human dynamic. Learning is essential to successfully deal with the human dynamic. Understanding our relationships and how we all learn in combination with other aspects of the matrix of four, particularly the four types of information, the four PaRDeS, the Analogy of the Divided Line and the Four Causes can be particularly revealing whenever any consideration arises in among our dynamic interactions.

Human history is probably the best subject to learn in order to better understand the human dynamic. The best way to look at reality is with some hindsight and learning history allows us to do just that. Learning human history is a serious endeavor, compromised of many ages and aspects, and fittingly can be summarized into four segments. There was the nomadic world, there was the hunter-gatherer world, the agricultural world and most recently the industrial world developed. We are in the fourth age of man. It is our choice to be open and giving or closed and uncaring in this world as far as how we interact with each other and our surroundings.

Whether one is in the company of historians in university or Hopi traditionalists at Prophecy Rock, it is obvious humankind and the entire world along with us, is on the cusp of a transition. It is apparent to many that our consciousness is developing and it is obvious to most the planet is changing. We might very well be making the transition to a technological/spiritual culture or an towards an environmentally degraded landscape allowing for little culture at all, or a various combination of the two. If indeed we are on the precipice of an end and a new beginning, no matter what it is, in order to make transition successfully, internally and externally, we have to be righteous rebels and take compassionate and conscious action. We have to be open and caring with our hearts and minds. We have to live and learn as well as love and teach.

"When one realizes one is asleep, at that moment one is already half awake."

~P.D. Ouspensky

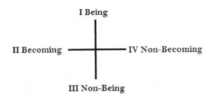

Living, loving, learning and teaching are like the cross reference set of four based on being and becoming. One can easily be in any one of these states of consciousness. At different times people all go through different phases or aspects and dwell in different levels as they are experiencing their own individual microcosmic stages or yugas, as expressed in the macrocosmic idea of the Kali Yuga, the cycle of time based on four celestial seasons. Individuals and collective societies go through these stages as does the whole planet. The matrix of four is part of the rhythm in the melody of universal balance. The matrix of four, the philosophy of the duality of polarity is a human dynamic which unites science and theology, inward individual consciousness and external society. It represents the ebb and flow of life.

Most people in most of society are non-being and non-becoming. As individuals we are frequently static and oblivious to it. And in society we frequently just glide along in the same static way, following the status quo within the collective and as individuals. Frequently we believe we understand and without doubt as to the validity of our sentiments, but like children or like a citizen in the Allegory of the Cave we are only seeing a small portion of reality.

145

Sometimes we are not even aware we are living this way. Many people spend most of their time doing things in attempts to settle any being or becoming for being and becoming is usually one tumultuous climb.

Being and becoming leads to awareness and sometimes relative hyperawareness compared to the dullness of non-being and non-becoming especially. Individually and society as a whole has to face itself when becoming and being and this can be upsetting to anyone. This is, I believe, is the main reason people would rather be busy at all times, making meditation difficult at all times.

Hakuin Ekaku, born in 1686 Japan, was one of the most influential figures in Zen Buddhism. He theorized four stages of knowing or learning as well. The four stages were simplified from the eight forms of consciousness coalescing into four upon attainment of a certain profound level of Zen mind state. The first stage formed from the first five forms of consciousness, more commonly understood as the five senses, and is called the perfection of action, based on the physical. The sixth consciousness breaks down into the second stage of mental cognition. The third is the perfection of the universal mind. And the fourth stage is called the great mirror mind, a combination of the prior three and a separate state on its own.

The four stages of knowing in Zen, as theorized by Hakuin Ekaku, are related to the four gates on the Buddhist path. The first gate is the inspiration to awaken. The second gate is the purification of practice. The third gate is the gate of awakening self so one can help others. And the fourth is the gate of Nirvana, knowing without defilement. Nirvana is the fourth state of peaceful elevated consciousness, the union of the three and the distinct part among them.

In all of these systems the fourth aspect is the unsaid supreme. We all have had intuitive hints now and then, intuitive events occur due to the accessing the fourth aspect. We all understand that there are three comprehensive aspects of time. We all know there is the past, present and future. And yet time itself is abstract and fluid ever unfolding and cascading with intuitive events that supersede time. Intuitive events are beyond past, present and future designation of time. Intuition arrives from the fourth unsaid aspect of time, that is timelessness or as the Tibetan Buddhists put it, 'time of no time.' Timelessness is the origin of intuition and the eminent abode of Nirvana.

We all have the opportunity to advance our consciousness, and we all have the capability of tapping into timelessness. We are all subject to cross the Four Rivers of life from Tibetan Buddhist conception. We all must face birth, old age, sickness and death, the four ultimate crossings of great difficulty. We are all here for a brief time, so why not choose to be like the fourth monkey, or the freed prisoner and help instead of hinder, to look, listen and speak in a righteous manner. Tibetan Buddhists note there are four devils to meditation and by extrapolation and alliteration, to happy life in general; illness, interruption, death and desires. Why would anyone want to bring such devilishness to anyone's meditation or anything in reality that would lead to any of these taking over? No fourth monkey would, and no freed prisoner would.

Buddha noted there are four Cooperative Acts or four actions, sometimes called the Bodhisattva's Virtues. They are giving things that others like to receive, saying things that others like to hear, doing profitable deeds for other sentient beings, and adapting under all circumstances for the benefit of all sentient beings. We can always choose to take responsible action in the form of one of the Cooperative Acts, no matter what.

Everything we are capable of doing is based on four functions, these four functions serve to liberate and excel ourselves and our surroundings, when in balance. When the four functions are not imbalanced, when one overrides the others, we might repeat misdirected patterns. These functions serve to either inhibit or excel. We operate via and are capable of emotion, thought, speech and action. Normally when people are out of balance it is rooted in the emotions, which in turn is cause for misdirected thinking, speech and actions or reactions.

"Mind precedes all mental states. Mind is their chief; they are all mind-wrought. If with a pure mind a person speaks or acts happiness follows him like his never-departing shadow." ~Buddha

"Happiness is when what you think, what you say, and what you do are in harmony." ~Gandhi

The Duality of Polarity

Where there is one, there is likely a contrasting polarity.

Where there is a single polarity, there is likely a second.

Where there are three, there is likely a fourth.

Where there are four, there is likely a duality of polarity.

Where there are four, there is likely one distinction.

Notes of Contrast

The epigraph attributed to Gandhi may be sourced from a speech by trade unionist Nicholas Klein. "First they ignore you. Then they ridicule you. And then they attack you and want to burn you. And then they build monuments to you. And that is what is going to happen to the Amalgamated Clothing Workers of America."

Six Paramitas (~transcendental actions): perfection of generosity, ethics, patience, enthusiastic perseverance, concentration, wisdom.

Noble Eightfold Path to Enlightenment: Right Understanding, Right Intent, Right Speech, Right Action, Right Livelihood, Right Effort, Right Mindfulness, and Right Concentration.

Zen Koan Learning Silence

The pupils of the Tendai School used to study meditation before Zen entered Japan. Four of them who were intimate friends promised one another to observe seven days of silence.

On the first day all were silent. Their meditation had begun auspiciously, but when night came and the oil lamps were growing dim one of the pupils could not help exclaiming to a servant, "Fix those lamps."

The second pupil was surprised to hear the first one talk. "We are not supposed to say a word," he remarked.

"You two are stupid. Why did you talk?" asked the third.

"I am the only one who has not talked," concluded the fourth pupil.

"The outward freedom that we shall attain will only be in exact proportion to the inward freedom to which we may have grown at a given moment. And if this is a correct view of freedom, our chief energy must be concentrated on achieving reform from within." ~Gandhi

"He who knows he who knows not, and knows not that he knows not, is a fool, shun him;

He who knows not, and knows that he knows not, is a child, teach him.

He who knows, and knows not that he knows, is asleep, wake him.

He who knows, and knows that he knows, is wise, follow him."

~Persian proverb

"The first question which the priest and the Levite asked was: 'If I stop to help this man, what will happen to me?' But...the good Samaritan reversed the question: 'If I do not stop to help this man, what will happen to him?'

~Martin Luther King Jr.

"You can speak. What other animal on the planet can speak? The word is the most powerful tool you have as a human; it is the tool of magic. But like a sword with two edges, your word can create the most beautiful dream, or your word can destroy everything around you. One edge is the misuse of the word, which creates a living hell. The other edge is the impeccability of the word, which will only create beauty, love, and heaven on Earth. Depending on how it is used the word can set you free, or it can enslave you more than you know." ~Don Miguel Ruiz, The Four Agreements

"A wise man can learn more from a foolish question than a fool can learn from a wise answer." ~Bruce Lee

Socrates described four virtues; prudence, courage, temperance and justice.

"Comfort the afflicted, afflict the comfortable." ~Finley Peter Dunne

"He who owns little is little owned." ~Henry David Thoreau

"Trifles make perfection, but perfection is no trifle." ~Michelangelo

"Ask not what your country can do for you, ask what you can do for your country." ~John F. Kennedy

"What is rational is real and what is real is rational." ~ Georg Wilhelm Hegel

"The great mass of the citizens become lovers of money...And so they grow richer and richer and the more they think of making a fortune they less they think of virtue. For when riches and virtue are placed together on the scales of the balance the one always rises as the other falls." ~Socrates

"Adversity makes men, prosperity makes monsters." ~Victor Hugo

"See friends in strangers and strangers in friends." ~Unknown

Fichtean dialectic considers critical thinking in four parts. Everything is transient and finite, existing in the medium of time. Everything is composed of contradictions. Gradual change leads to crises, turning points when one force overcomes its opposing force. Change is helical, not circular.

"Man is a machine which reacts blindly to external forces and, this being so, he has no will, and very little control of himself, if any at all. What we have to study, therefore, is not psychology-for that applies only to a developed man-but mechanics. Man is not only a machine but a machine which works very much below the standard it would be capable of maintaining if it were working properly." ~P. D. Ouspensky

Someone knocked on the door.

"Who is it?"

"It is me." The lover answered.

"Go away."

Lover returns and knocks again. "Who is it?"

"It is I."

"Go away."

Lover returns much later and knocks again. "Who is it?"

"It is I. And I have spent the last year knowledge and wealth."

"Go away."

After sometime he returns again. "Who is it?"

"It is you."

And the lover opened the door.

~Sufi Parable

"Great doubt: great awakening. Little doubt: little awakening. No doubt: no awakening."

~Zen Koan

"Love the life you live, live the life you love." ~Bob Marley

"When you were born, you cried and the world rejoiced. Live your life so that when you die, the world cries and you rejoice." ~Cherokee proverb

"Those who know don't talk. Those who talk don't know." ~Lao Tzu

"In some ways it is.

In some ways it is not.

In some ways it is and is not.

In some ways it is and it is indescribable.

In some ways it is not and it is indescribable.

In some ways it is, it is not and it is indescribable.

In some ways it is indescribable."

~Sevenfold Predication of Jainism

Buddha described four good friends:

Young man, be aware of these four good-hearted friends: the helper, the friend who endures in good times and bad, the mentor, and the compassionate friend. The helper can be identified by four things: by protecting you when you are vulnerable, and likewise your wealth, being a refuge when you are afraid, and in various tasks providing double what is requested. The enduring friend can be identified by four things: by telling you secrets, guarding your own secrets closely, not abandoning you in misfortune, and even dying for you. The mentor can be identified by four things: by restraining you from wrongdoing, guiding you towards good actions, telling you what you ought to know, and showing you the path to heaven [lasting happiness]. The compassionate friend can be identified by four things: by not rejoicing in your misfortune, delighting in your good fortune, preventing others from speaking ill of you, and encouraging others who praise your good qualities.

Buddha also described four enemies disguised as friends:

Young man, be aware of these four enemies disguised as friends: the taker, the talker, the flatterer, and the reckless companion. The taker can be identified by four things: by only taking, asking for a lot while giving little, performing duty out of fear, and offering service in order to gain something. The talker can be identified by four things: by reminding of past generosity, promising future generosity, mouthing empty words of kindness, and protesting personal misfortune when called on to help. The flatterer can be identified by four things: by supporting both bad and good behavior indiscriminately, praising you to your face, and putting you down behind your back. The reckless companion can be identified by four things: by accompanying you in drinking, roaming around at night, partying, and gambling.

Blessed are the poor in spirit: for theirs is the kingdom of heaven.

Blessed are they that mourn: for they shall be comforted.

Blessed are the meek: for they shall inherit the Earth.

Blessed are they which do hunger and thirst after righteousness: for they shall be filled.

Blessed are the merciful: for they shall obtain mercy.

Blessed are the pure in heart: for they shall see God.

Blessed are the peacemakers: for they shall be called the children of God,

Blessed are they which are persecuted for righteousness' sake: for theirs is the kingdom of heaven.

~Eight Beatitudes of Jesus

"As the biggest library if it is in disorder is not as useful as a small but well-arranged one, so you may accumulate a vast amount of knowledge but it will be of far less value than a much smaller amount if you have not thought it over for yourself." ~Arthur Schopenhauer

"Everything exists: that is one extreme. Everything doesn't exist: that is another extreme. Avoiding these two extremes the Tathagata teaches the Dhamma via the middle." ~Basic concept of The Middle Way

167. Do not follow the evil law! Do not live on in thoughtlessness! Do not follow false doctrine! Be not a friend of the world.

168. Rouse thyself! Do not be idle! Follow the law of virtue! The virtuous rests in bliss in this world and in the next.

169. Follow the law of virtue; do not follow that of sin. The virtuous rests in bliss in this world and in the next.

170. Look upon the world as a bubble, look upon it as a mirage: the king of death does not see him who thus looks down upon the world.

171. Come, look at this glittering world, like unto a royal chariot; the foolish are immersed in it, but the wise do not touch it.

172. He who formerly was reckless and afterwards became sober, brightens up this world, like the moon when freed from clouds.

173. He whose evil deeds are covered by good deeds, brightens up this world, like the moon when freed from clouds.

174. This world is dark, few only can see here; a few only go to heaven, like birds escaped from the net.

175. The swans go on the path of the sun, they go through the ether by means of their miraculous power; the wise are led out of this world, when they have conquered Mara and his train.

176. If a man has transgressed one law, and speaks lies, and scoffs at another world, there is no evil he will not do.

177. The uncharitable do not go to the world of the gods; fools only do not praise liberality; a wise man rejoices in liberality, and through it becomes blessed in the other world.

178. Better than sovereignty over the Earth, better than going to heaven, better than lordship over all worlds, is the reward of the first step in holiness."

~The chapter The World from the Dhammapada (words of the Buddha)

When we look at modern man, we have to face the fact that modern man suffers from a kind of poverty of the spirit, which stands in glaring contrast to his scientific and technological abundance; We've learned to fly the air like birds, we've learned to swim the seas like fish, and yet we haven't learned to walk the Earth as brothers and sisters."

~Martin Luther King Jr.

The four cardinal virtues of Christianity are prudence, justice, temperance, and fortitude.

The four cardinal virtues of Hinduism are non-violence, truth, purity and self-control.

The following sets of four are all celebrated in Buddhism: The Four Mental Principles are wisdom, truthfulness, abandonment of evil and selfishness, and appeasement. The Four Bases of Success are appreciation, effort, attention and investigation. The Four Divine States of Mind are loving-kindness, compassion, sympathetic joy over others' achievement and equanimity. The Four Virtues Conducive to Social Welfare are generosity, kind speech, benevolence and adaptability. The Fourfold Right Effort is made up of the effort to restrain from evil the effort to abandon evil, the effort to develop good and the effort to maintain good.

"The more real you get, the more unreal everything else is."

~John Lennon

May all sentient beings have happiness and its causes,

May all sentient beings be free of suffering and its causes,

May all sentient beings never be separated from bliss without suffering,

May all sentient beings be in equanimity, free of bias, attachment and anger.

~Prayer for the Four Immeasurables of Buddhism; Love, Compassion, Joy and Equanimity

~Please leave a review on amazon.com for the *Matrix of Four, The Philosophy of The Duality of Polarity*. Reviews make all the difference for an independent author and philosopher.

For further reading, Ethan Indigo Smith's *The Geometry of Energy How to Meditate* and *108 Steps to Be in The Zone*, both directly inspired by *The Matrix of Four*. Ethan also penned *The Terraist Letters, The Printed Threat* and *The Complete Patriot's Guide to Oligarchical Collectivism*.

Made in the USA
Monee, IL
01 May 2021